Dinner and Supper Parties

HAMLYN

LONDON · NEW YORK · SYDNEY · TORONTO

Acknowledgements
Recipes created by Diana Jaggar
Photography by John Lee
Cover picture by Iain Reid
Artwork by John Scott Martin
China kindly loaned by Royal Doulton Tableware Limited,
Denby Tableware Limited and David Mellor

Published by
The Hamlyn Publishing Group Limited
London · New York · Sydney · Toronto
Astronaut House, Feltham, Middlesex, England

ISBN 0 600 32936 4

Printed in Spain by Printer industria gráfica sa
Sant Vicenç dels Horts   Barcelona   1978
Depósito Legal B. 12429-1978

Contents

Introduction

Useful facts and figures

Entertaining, whether giving an informal fork buffet or a more sophisticated dinner party, can be great fun for the hostess as well as her guests. The secret of success is careful planning and preparation beforehand, enabling the hostess to spend more time with her guests and less in the kitchen.

In this book there is a wide variety of exciting and unusual recipes for you to choose from. Bear in mind a few simple rules when planning your dinner or supper party menu. First of all, take into consideration the number of people, the size of your dining area and the occasion you are planning for. Never serve two similar foods in the same menu. For example, if you are serving a cheesecake for a dessert, do not serve a starter with cheese; avoid a fish starter followed by a main fish course, or serving too many dishes with rich sauces. Textures of food are important – try to include both soft and crisp textures and take advantage of fruit and vegetables in season when they are at their best, and also cheapest. If you own a freezer, make full use of it by preparing soups, casseroles and bases for desserts well in advance.

It is always useful to make a count-down plan, so that you can see at a glance what has to be done and avoid any last minute panics.

Good food deserves a good wine to accompany it. The choice of wine is basically a matter of personal taste, but there are certain guidelines which may be followed. A dry white wine is usually considered best to serve with fish and white meats such as chicken, pork and veal, whereas a red wine is normally served with all red meats and game. A sweet white wine is a perfect accompaniment to desserts. If in doubt, it is a good idea to have a chat with your local wine merchant who will be pleased to help you in choosing the appropriate wine or wines to complement your menu. Remember that any dish cooked in wine should be accompanied by the same type of wine.

Red wine needs time to breathe before it is ready for drinking. Remove the cork a few hours before the wine is to be served and decant if wished. Serve red wines at room temperature and white and rose wines chilled, but not icy – usually an hour in the refrigerator is sufficient.

Notes on metrication

In this book quantities are given in metric, imperial and American measures. Exact conversion from imperial to metric measures does not usually give very convenient working quantities and so the metric measures have been rounded off into units of 25 grams. The table below shows the recommended equivalents.

Ounces	Approx. g to nearest whole figure	Recommended conversion to nearest unit of 25
1	28	25
2	57	50
3	85	75
4	113	100
5	142	150
6	170	175
7	198	200
8	227	225
9	255	250
10	283	275
11	312	300
12	340	350
13	368	375
14	397	400
15	425	425
16 (1 lb)	454	450
17	482	475
18	510	500
19	539	550
20	567	575

Note: When converting quantities over 20 oz first add the appropriate figures in the centre column, then adjust to the nearest unit of 25. As a general guide, 1 kg (1000 g) equals 2.2 lb or about 2 lb 3 oz. This method of conversion gives good results in nearly all cases but in certain pastry and cake recipes a more accurate conversion is necessary to produce a balanced recipe. On the other hand, quantities of such ingredients as vegetables, fruit, meat and fish which are not critical are rounded off to the nearest quarter of a kg as this is how they are likely to be purchased.

Liquid measures The millilitre has been used in this book and the following table gives a few examples:

Imperial	Approx. ml to nearest whole figure	Recommended ml
$\frac{1}{4}$ pint	142	150 ml
$\frac{1}{2}$ pint	283	300 ml
$\frac{3}{4}$ pint	425	450 ml
1 pint	567	600 ml
1$\frac{1}{2}$ pints	851	900 ml
1$\frac{3}{4}$ pints	992	1000 ml (1 litre)

Note: For quantities of 1$\frac{3}{4}$ pints and over we have used litres and fractions of a litre.

Spoon measures All spoon measures given in this book are level.

Can sizes At present, cans are marked with the exact (usually to the nearest whole number) metric equivalent of the imperial weight of the contents, so we have followed this practice when giving can sizes.

Oven temperatures

The table below gives recommended equivalents.

	°F	°C	Gas Mark
Very cool	225	110	$\frac{1}{4}$
	250	120	$\frac{1}{2}$
Cool	275	140	1
	300	150	2
Moderate	325	160	3
	350	180	4
Moderately hot	375	190	5
	400	200	6
Hot	425	220	7
	450	230	8
Very hot	475	240	9

Note: When making any of the recipes in this book, only follow one set of measures as they are not interchangeable.

Notes for American users

Although the recipes in this book give American measures, the lists below give some equivalents or substitutes for terms and commodities which may be unfamiliar to American readers.

Equipment and terms
BRITISH/AMERICAN

cake or loaf tin/cake or loaf pan
cling film/Saran wrap
cocktail stick/toothpick
flan tin/pie pan
frying pan/skillet
greaseproof paper/waxed paper
grill/broil
kitchen paper/paper towels

liquidise/blend
mince/grind
packet/package
piping bag/pastry bag
polythene/plastic
roasting tin/roasting pan
sandwich tin/layer cake pan
stoned/pitted

Ingredients
BRITISH/AMERICAN

arrowroot/arrowroot flour
aubergine/eggplant
bacon rashers/bacon slices
beef fillet/beef tenderloin
beetroot/beet
belly pork/salt pork
black cherries/Bing cherries
black olives/ripe olives
castor or granulated sugar/sugar
chicory/Belgian endive
cooking apples/baking apples
cornflour/cornstarch
courgettes/zucchini
double cream/heavy cream
essence/extract
gammon steaks/bacon steaks
gherkin/sweet dill pickle
glacé cherry/candied cherry
ham/cured or smoked ham

hard-boiled eggs/hardcooked eggs
icing sugar/confectioners' sugar
ketchup/catsup
lard/shortening
offal/variety meats
plain chocolate/semi-sweet chocolate
plain flour/all-purpose flour
plain yogurt/unflavored yogurt
puff pastry/puff paste
shortcrust pastry/basic pie dough
single cream/light cream
sponge finger biscuits/lady fingers
spring onion/scallion
sultanas/seedless white raisins
tomato purée/tomato paste
topside of beef/top round of beef
unsalted butter/sweet butter
veal escalopes/veal scallops

Note: The British and Australian pint is 20 fluid ounces as opposed to the American pint which is 16 fluid ounces.

Notes for Australian users

Ingredients in this book are given in cup, metric and imperial measures. In Australia the American 8-oz measuring cup is used in conjunction with the imperial pint of 20 fluid ounces. It is most important to remember that the Australian tablespoon differs from both the British and American tablespoons; the table below gives a comparison between the standard tablespoons used in the three countries. The British standard tablespoon holds 17.7 millilitres, the American 14.2 millilitres, and the Australian 20 millilitres. A teaspoon holds approximately 5 millilitres in all three countries.

British	American	Australian
1 teaspoon	1 teaspoon	1 teaspoon
1 tablespoon	1 tablespoon	1 tablespoon
2 tablespoons	3 tablespoons	2 tablespoons
3$\frac{1}{2}$ tablespoons	4 tablespoons	3 tablespoons
4 tablespoons	5 tablespoons	3$\frac{1}{2}$ tablespoons

Soups and starters

In this chapter you will find an exciting variety of soup and starter recipes to choose from. Plan your starter so it is not too filling or too over-powering. Try to choose foods such as melons and avocados when they are in season.

Soups are always enhanced by garnishes, such as croûtons or swirls of cream for that extra touch of luxury. There are some interesting ideas for cold soups, perfect for those summer dinner parties. The more unusual fish soups are really to be recommended, although it is advisable to make the ones that use shellfish in the summer months when they can be bought fresh.

Prawn bisque

METRIC/IMPERIAL/AMERICAN
scant 1.5 litres/2½ pints/6¼ cups whole prawns
225 g/8 oz/½ lb sole bones and trimmings for stock
pared rind of ½ lemon
1 bay leaf
parsley stalks
few peppercorns
225 g/8 oz/2 cups onion, finely chopped
40 g/1½ oz/3 tablespoons butter
25 g/1 oz/¼ cup plain flour
cayenne pepper
100 ml/4 fl oz/½ cup white wine
½ teaspoon anchovy essence
chopped parsley to garnish

Peel the prawns, reserving 6 for garnish with just the body shell removed. Put the shells in a pan with the sole bones and trimmings, 2.25 litres/4 pints/5 pints water, lemon rind, bay leaf, parsley stalks and peppercorns. Bring to the boil and simmer for 20 minutes. Strain, return to the pan and boil to reduce by half.

Sauté the onion in the butter, add the flour and cook for 1 minute; gradually add the reduced fish stock. Whisk until smooth. Season with salt, pepper and cayenne, bring to the boil and simmer for 15 minutes. Add the wine, anchovy essence and peeled prawns. Garnish each bowl with a prawn and parsley.

Serves 6

Soupe de poisson Espagnole

METRIC/IMPERIAL/AMERICAN
225 g/8 oz/½ lb haddock or whiting fillet
750 ml/1¼ pints/3 cups fish stock
bouquet garni
1 clove garlic, crushed
pinch thyme
200 ml/8 fl oz/1 cup dry white wine
generous litre/1 quart/5 cups mussels, prepared
1 onion, finely chopped
25 g/1 oz/2 tablespoons butter
20 g/¾ oz/2½ tablespoons plain flour
1 canned pimento, sliced
pinch powdered saffron
2 egg yolks
150 ml/¼ pint/⅔ cup single cream

Poach the haddock in the stock with the bouquet garni for 15 minutes. Discard the bouquet garni, remove the skin and bones from the fish and liquidise the fish and stock. Boil the garlic, thyme and wine in a pan. Add the prepared mussels and toss, with the pan lid on, for 2–3 minutes until the mussels are just beginning to open. Strain the stock. Shell the mussels.

Sauté the onion in the butter, add the flour, fish and mussel stocks, and pimento. Bring to the boil, whisking. Add the saffron, salt and pepper, and simmer for 10 minutes. Blend the egg yolks and cream, whisk into the pan with the mussels. Heat without boiling. Garnish and serve with croûtons.

Serves 6

Mushroom consommé

METRIC/IMPERIAL/AMERICAN
350 g/12 oz/3 cups button mushrooms, washed
225 g/8 oz/2 cups onions, finely chopped
40 g/1½ oz/3 tablespoons butter
25 g/1 oz/¼ cup plain flour
generous litre/2 pints/5 cups strong chicken stock
2 tablespoons/2 tablespoons/3 tablespoons mushroom
    ketchup (optional)
1 bay leaf
1 teaspoon chopped fresh tarragon
salt and freshly ground pepper
chopped parsley to garnish

Trim the mushroom stalks and chop finely. Slice mushroom caps thinly. Soften the onion in the butter with the chopped mushroom stalks. Add the flour and cook for 1–2 minutes. Gradually stir in the stock and bring to the boil. Add the ketchup, bay leaf, tarragon and the sliced mushrooms. Season and cover and simmer for 15–20 minutes. Remove the bay leaf. Adjust the seasoning and serve sprinkled with parsley and garnished with a few slices of mushroom.
Note: A bunch of very finely chopped watercress may be added 5 minutes before the end of the cooking time, and 300 ml/½ pint/1¼ cups single cream added before serving the soup hot or chilled.

Serves 6

Spicy tomato and pepper soup

METRIC/IMPERIAL/AMERICAN
1 onion, sliced
50 g/2 oz/¼ cup butter
15 g/½ oz/2 tablespoons flour
450 g/1 lb/1 lb ripe tomatoes, washed and quartered
750 ml/1¼ pints/3 cups chicken stock
1 blade mace
6 peppercorns
2 cloves
1 teaspoon paprika
1 bay leaf
pared rind of ½ lemon
salt and freshly ground pepper
225 g/8 oz/½ lb red peppers, finely chopped
100 ml/4 fl oz/½ cup port or red wine
1 teaspoon chopped fresh basil or parsley to garnish

Sauté the onion in half the butter, add the flour and cook for 1 minute. Add the tomatoes, stock, spices, bay leaf, lemon rind and seasoning. Bring to the boil, cover the pan and simmer gently for 20 minutes.

Meanwhile, soften the red pepper in the remaining butter, then strain the tomato mixture into this pan and bring to the boil. Simmer gently for a further 10 minutes. Add the port, adjust the seasoning and serve in individual bowls. Garnish.

Serves 6

Iced tomato, cucumber and mint soup

METRIC/IMPERIAL/AMERICAN
50 g/2 oz/¼ cup butter
225 g/8 oz/2 cups onions, chopped
1 kg/2 lb/2 lb ripe tomatoes, washed and quartered
1 small cucumber, peeled and chopped
2 bay leaves
pinch dried basil
pinch sugar
salt and freshly ground pepper
1 litre/1¾ pints/4¼ cups chicken stock
1 mint sprig
3 tablespoons/3 tablespoons/¼ cup sherry
1 tablespoon chopped mint
mint sprigs to garnish

Melt the butter in a pan. Add the onions, tomatoes, cucumber, herbs, sugar and seasoning. Sauté gently in the covered pan for 15 minutes. Add the stock and sprig of mint and simmer for 10 minutes. Either liquidise and sieve, or sieve the tomato mixture. Add the sherry and leave to cool. Add the chopped mint, adjust the seasoning and chill thoroughly. To serve, put 2–3 ice cubes into each soup bowl and ladle the soup over. Garnish with sprigs of mint.

Serves 6

Chilled avocado and crab soup

METRIC/IMPERIAL/AMERICAN
2 ripe avocado pears
juice of 1 lemon
100 g/4 oz/$\frac{1}{4}$ lb crabmeat
300 ml/$\frac{1}{2}$ pint/1$\frac{1}{4}$ cups chicken stock
450 ml/16 fl oz/2 cups plain yogurt
1 teaspoon Worcestershire sauce
few drops Tabasco sauce
salt and freshly ground pepper

Halve, peel and quarter the avocados. Slice thinly and dip completely in lemon juice reserving a few slices for garnish. Place a little of this mixture in a covered bowl in the refrigerator. Put the remainder, together with the crabmeat, stock and yogurt into a liquidiser and blend until very smooth. Add Worcestershire sauce, Tabasco and seasoning to taste. Chill thoroughly. Before serving, stir the reserved avocado into the soup. Place 1 or 2 ice cubes into each bowl and add the soup. Float the reserved avocado slices on top.
Note: Broken crab claws may be carefully cracked and the whole pieces of crabmeat from each used to garnish the soup for a special occasion.

Serves 6

Iced cherry soup Chantilly

METRIC/IMPERIAL/AMERICAN
1 kg/2$\frac{1}{4}$ lb/2$\frac{1}{4}$ lb fresh black cherries, stalks removed
generous litre/2 pints/5 cups water
pared rind and juice of 1 orange
1 cinnamon stick
225 g/8 oz/1 cup castor sugar
300 ml/$\frac{1}{2}$ pint/1$\frac{1}{4}$ cups sweet red wine
3 tablespoons/3 tablespoons/$\frac{1}{4}$ cup arrowroot
GARNISH:
150 ml/$\frac{1}{4}$ pint/$\frac{2}{3}$ cup soured cream
50 g/2 oz/$\frac{1}{2}$ cup flaked almonds

Reserving 100 g/4 oz/$\frac{1}{4}$ lb whole cherries, gently simmer the remainder with the water, orange rind and juice and cinnamon stick for 20 minutes. Strain the juices into a clean pan, pressing the cherries very well. Add the sugar and bring slowly to the boil. Stone the remaining cherries over a basin to reserve the juices. Add these to the pan with the wine. Thicken with the arrowroot blended with a little cold water and bring to the boil for 1 minute. Leave to cool, then chill thoroughly. Serve cold with a spoonful of soured cream on each serving and a few flaked almonds.

Serves 6

Eggs Jacqueline

METRIC/IMPERIAL/AMERICAN

3 hard-boiled eggs, halved lengthwise
25 g/1 oz/2 tablespoons softened butter
100 g/4 oz/⅔ cup peeled prawns
paprika
225 g/8 oz/½ lb asparagus, trimmed, cooked and cut in
    4-cm/1½-inch/1½-inch pieces
25 g/1 oz/¼ cup Parmesan cheese, grated
watercress to garnish
BÉCHAMEL SAUCE:
20 g/¾ oz/1½ tablespoons butter
20 g/¾ oz/3 tablespoons flour
300 ml/½ pint/1¼ cups flavoured milk (infused with slice
    of onion, bay leaf and peppercorns)

Remove the egg yolks and sieve into a bowl. Mix with butter
and 25 g/1 oz/2 tablespoons of chopped prawns. Season with
paprika, salt and pepper. Spoon mixture into the whites and
sandwich. Put the asparagus into the base of 6 ovenproof
ramekin dishes. Place eggs on top and add remaining prawns.

Make béchamel sauce: melt butter in a small pan and stir in
the flour. Cook for 1 minute then gradually add the flavoured
milk and bring to the boil. Simmer for 2 minutes and season to
taste. Spoon over the eggs, sprinkle with cheese and cook in a
moderate oven (180°C, 350°F, Gas Mark 4) for 15–20 minutes
until well browned. Garnish with watercress.

Serves 6

Moules farcies Bretonne

METRIC/IMPERIAL/AMERICAN

generous litre/2 quarts/5 cups large mussels
225 g/8 oz/1 cup unsalted butter
1 large onion, finely chopped
3 cloves garlic, crushed
1 tablespoon chopped parsley
50 g/2 oz/1 cup fresh white breadcrumbs
40 g/1½ oz/⅓ cup grated Parmesan cheese
100 ml/4 fl oz/½ cup dry white wine

Wash and scrub the mussel shells under cold water. Remove
beards and discard any open shells. Place the mussels in a
steamer or colander over a pan of boiling water. Cover with a
lid and steam for 2–3 minutes until the shells just open. Do not
overcook. Stir to ensure all shells are steamed. Remove from
the heat. Break off the empty half of each shell and place the
filled halves on a board.

Cream the butter with the onion, garlic, parsley and pepper.
Spread a little into each shell and arrange close together in 6
individual ovenproof gratin dishes or one large ovenproof dish.
Sprinkle with breadcrumbs and cheese mixed together and
spoon over the wine. Chill.

Place the dish on a baking sheet and cover with foil. Cook for
15–20 minutes at the top of a moderate oven (180°C, 350°F, Gas
Mark 4). Remove the foil and continue cooking for a further
5 minutes to brown. Serve with French bread.

Serves 6

Gratin au fruits de mer

METRIC/IMPERIAL/AMERICAN
350 g/12 oz/¾ lb cod fillet, skinned and cut into strips
100–150 g/4–6 oz/¾–1 cup peeled prawns
6 scallops, cut into quarters
juice of 1 lemon
salt and pepper
1 small onion, finely chopped
50 g/2 oz/¼ cup butter
100 ml/4 fl oz/½ cup white wine
40 g/1½ oz/6 tablespoons plain flour
450 ml/¾ pint/2 cups milk, infused with 1 bay leaf,
    1 blade mace and peppercorns
25 g/1 oz/¼ cup grated Parmesan cheese
parsley sprigs to garnish

Mix the cod strips, prawns and scallops with the lemon juice and seasoning. Divide between 6 deep scallop shells or ovenproof dishes. Sauté the onion in the butter then add the wine and bring to the boil. Simmer until reduced by half before whisking in the flour. Cook until smooth, stirring continuously. Strain in the infused milk and bring back to the boil. Simmer for 2–3 minutes. Adjust the seasoning and spoon over the fish to cover. Sprinkle with cheese. Bake at the top of a moderately hot oven (190°C, 375°F, Gas Mark 5) for 20–30 minutes until golden brown on top. Garnish with parsley sprigs.
Note: Scampi, halibut or nuggets of firm white fish mixed with some sliced mushrooms can be used as an alternative.

Serves 6

Prawn soufflés

METRIC/IMPERIAL/AMERICAN
20 g/¾ oz/1½ tablespoons butter
1 teaspoon paprika
600 ml/1 pint/2½ cups shelled prawns
few drops Tabasco sauce
450 ml/¾ pint/2 cups béchamel sauce (see method)
2 tablespoons/2 tablespoons/3 tablespoons cream
3 egg yolks
4 egg whites
little grated cheese mixed with browned breadcrumbs

Melt the butter in a large pan and add the paprika. Cook for 1 minute then add the prawns, Tabasco, salt and pepper. Add the prepared béchamel sauce and cream and mix well. For the béchamel sauce, melt 40 g/1½ oz/3 tablespoons butter in a pan. Stir in 40 g/1½ oz/6 tablespoons flour and cook for 1 minute. Gradually add 450 ml/¾ pint/2 cups milk which has been infused with 1 bay leaf, 1 blade of mace and a slice of onion and then strained. Bring to the boil for 2 minutes and season to taste.

Cool slightly then beat in the egg yolks thoroughly, one at a time. Whisk the egg whites until stiff but not dry and stir 1 tablespoon into the mixture. Carefully fold in the remainder. Spoon into 6 individual ovenproof soufflé dishes, place on a baking sheet and sprinkle with the cheese and breadcrumb mixture. Bake in a moderate oven (180°C, 350°F, Gas Mark 4) for 20–25 minutes until firm. Serve immediately.

Serves 6

Ogen melon with mint ice

METRIC/IMPERIAL/AMERICAN
MINT ICE:
450 ml/¾ pint/2 cups water
100 g/4 oz/½ cup sugar
pared rind and juice of 2 lemons
large handful of fresh mint
few drops of green food colouring

3 small ogen melons, chilled

Boil the water, sugar and pared lemon rinds for 5 minutes. Remove from the heat and add the mint. Infuse for 10 minutes then add the lemon juice. Strain and add colouring sparingly. Cool, then freeze until firm. Whisk with an electric beater or use a liquidiser. Return to the freezer until firm.

To serve, cut the melons in half, open and discard the seeds. Pile spoonfuls of the mint ice into the centre of each melon and decorate with crystallised mint leaves, if liked. Serve at once.

(To crystallise mint leaves, pick the small tips of the mint only. Brush sparingly with egg white and dip in sugar until completely coated. Lay on a metal sheet and freeze until crisp.)
Note: Mint ice is also delicious served with grapefruit.

Serves 6

Avocado mousse ring

METRIC/IMPERIAL/AMERICAN
3 ripe avocado pears
juice of 1 lemon
2 tablespoons/2 tablespoons/3 tablespoons French
   dressing
25 g/1 oz/2 envelopes powdered gelatine
150 ml/¼ pint/⅔ cup chicken stock
150 ml/¼ pint/⅔ cup dry white wine
150 ml/¼ pint/⅔ cup thick mayonnaise
150 ml/¼ pint/⅔ cup double cream, whipped
1 teaspoon onion juice
2 teaspoons Worcestershire sauce
GARNISH:
600 ml/1 pint/2½ cups whole unshelled prawns
1 bunch watercress, washed and picked into sprigs

Peel and slice the avocado pears. Mix with the lemon juice and French dressing and leave to marinate for 30 minutes. Liquidise or sieve to make 450 ml/¾ pint/2 cups purée. Meanwhile, soak the gelatine in a little of the chicken stock in a basin and dissolve over a pan of hot water. Add the remaining stock and the white wine. Add the mayonnaise and cream to the avocado purée with onion juice and Worcestershire sauce. Stir in gelatine mixture evenly and add salt and pepper. Turn into an oiled 23-cm/9-inch ring mould. Cover with cling film and chill until set. Meanwhile remove the body shells from prawns.

To serve, turn the mousse out on to a flat serving dish. Arrange the prawns around and fill the centre with watercress.

Serves 6

Devilled stuffed avocado pears

METRIC/IMPERIAL/AMERICAN
STUFFING:
150 ml/¼ pint/⅔ cup French dressing
1 tablespoon Worcestershire sauce
½ teaspoon French mustard
1 teaspoon tomato purée
few drops Tabasco sauce
pinch sugar
salt and freshly ground pepper
1 large red pepper, diced
2 spring onions, trimmed, washed and shredded
4 tomatoes, skinned, deseeded and chopped

3 large ripe avocado pears
juice of 1 lemon
lemon twists to garnish

Prepare the stuffing by mixing the French dressing, Worcester-shire sauce, mustard, tomato purée, Tabasco and sugar in a bowl. Season to taste. Add the pepper, onions and tomatoes.

Halve the avocados and discard the stones. Wipe over the surface of each half with lemon juice and spoon the devilled stuffing into the centres. Garnish each with a twist of lemon. Serve chilled.
Note: A little curry sauce may be added to the filling.

Serves 6

Eggs niçoise

METRIC/IMPERIAL/AMERICAN
6 hard-boiled eggs
1 (56-g/2-oz/2-oz) can anchovy fillets, drained and soaked
    in milk
75 g/3 oz/6 tablespoons unsalted butter
freshly ground pepper
225 g/8 oz/½ lb French beans, cooked and cut into
    2.5-cm/1-inch/1-inch pieces
225 g/8 oz/½ lb tomatoes, skinned, quartered and
    deseeded
75–100 g/3–4 oz/½ cup black olives
garlic-flavoured French dressing
2 teaspoons finely chopped fresh herbs
300 ml/½ pint/1¼ cups thick mayonnaise
little cream or top of milk

Cut the eggs in half and remove and sieve the yolks. Reserve 6 anchovy fillets and mash the remainder with the egg yolks and butter until smooth. Season to taste and spoon the mixture back into the egg whites.

Mix the beans, tomatoes and olives with enough dressing to moisten. Place in a serving dish and arrange the eggs down the centre. Add the herbs to the mayonnaise and thin to a coating consistency with a little cream. Spoon carefully over the eggs to cover completely. Split the reserved anchovy fillets in half lengthwise and arrange in a cross on each egg.

Serves 6

Crab salad Margareta

METRIC/IMPERIAL/AMERICAN
4 hard-boiled eggs
225 g/8 oz/½ lb crabmeat
350 g/12 oz/¾ lb tomatoes, sliced and cut in half
1 medium cucumber, peeled and thinly sliced
3 anchovy fillets, drained and cut in half lengthwise
DRESSING:
4 tablespoons/4 tablespoons/⅓ cup oil
1 tablespoon wine vinegar
½ clove garlic, crushed
1 teaspoon French mustard
1 teaspoon paprika
2 tablespoons/2 tablespoons/3 tablespoons tomato
   chutney
lemon juice to taste
2 tablespoons/2 tablespoons/3 tablespoons cream
salt and freshly ground pepper

Cut the eggs in half, remove the yolks and chop the whites. Place the chopped egg white in the centre of a serving plate. Pile the crabmeat over and sieve the egg yolks around. Place the slices of tomato around the edge, then surround with cucumber slices.

   Mix the dressing ingredients together in a screw-topped jar, season to taste and spoon over the salad. Arrange a lattice of anchovy fillets on top of the crabmeat. Chill for 1 hour before serving with hot French bread.

Serves 6

Salmon and prawn mousse

METRIC/IMPERIAL/AMERICAN
350 g/12 oz/¾ lb fresh salmon
50 g/2 oz/¼ cup butter
BÉCHAMEL SAUCE:
300 ml/½ pint/1¼ cups flavoured milk (see page 12)
20 g/¾ oz/1½ tablespoons butter
20 g/¾ oz/3 tablespoons plain flour

150 ml/¼ pint/⅔ cup good mayonnaise
150 ml/¼ pint/⅔ cup double cream, whipped
50–75 g/2–3 oz/½ cup peeled prawns, roughly chopped
15 g/½ oz/1 envelope powdered gelatine
3 tablespoons/3 tablespoons/¼ cup fish stock or dry white
   wine
1 egg white, stiffly whisked
2 whole prawns and parsley sprig to garnish

Place the salmon on well-buttered foil and package loosely. Cook in a moderate oven (160°C, 325°F, Gas Mark 3) for 20 minutes. Remove from oven and cool in the foil. Remove skin and bones and flake the fish, reserving juices.

   Make up the béchamel sauce (see page 12), adding the fish juices, bring to the boil for 2 minutes and then cool. Beat in the salmon, mayonnaise, cream and prawns. Dissolve the gelatine in the stock in a basin over a pan of hot water, then add to the mixture. Fold in the egg white evenly and spoon into a fluted mould or individual ramekin dishes. Smooth the surface and chill until set. Garnish with prawns and parsley.

Serves 6

Danish smoked mackerel mousse with cucumber rolls

METRIC/IMPERIAL/AMERICAN
3 large lemons, washed
1 small smoked mackerel
150 ml/¼ pint/⅔ cup warm aspic jelly
1 egg, separated
150 ml/¼ pint/⅔ cup double cream, whipped
salt and freshly ground pepper
1 small jar Danish lumpfish caviar
watercress to garnish

Cut the lemons in half lengthwise and scoop out all the flesh, using a grapefruit knife. Leave the shells to drain. (Keep the juice from the flesh in the refrigerator for future use.) Skin the mackerel and remove all the bones. Add the still warm aspic jelly and egg yolk and blend in a liquidiser until smooth. Leave to cool.

Add the cream, season to taste and sharpen with some of the lemon juice. Fold in the stiffly whisked egg white and when the mousse begins to thicken, spoon into the lemon shells. Chill until set then pile a teaspoon of Danish caviar on each serving and garnish with watercress. Serve with matchsticks of cucumber wrapped in slices of buttered brown bread.

Serves 6

Coupe Indienne

METRIC/IMPERIAL/AMERICAN
1 ripe melon, chilled, halved and deseeded
225 g/8 oz/1¼ cups large peeled prawns
1 small red pepper, halved, cored and deseeded
1 small green pepper, halved, cored and deseeded
300 ml/½ pint/1¼ cups thick mayonnaise
1 tablespoon tomato ketchup
150 ml/¼ pint/⅔ cup double cream, whipped
½–1 teaspoon thick curry sauce, according to taste
1 teaspoon lemon juice
salt and pepper
4 whole prawns to garnish

Using a baller, scoop the melon flesh into balls, or cut into cubes. Mix with the prawns and peppers. Chill. Mix together the mayonnaise, ketchup and cream and stir in enough curry sauce to taste. Sharpen with the lemon juice and adjust seasoning. Stir into the melon mixture and serve in individual glasses. Peel the body shells from the prawns for garnishing and hang over the edge of the glasses before serving.
Note: If small ogen melons are available, this cocktail may be served in the melon shells.

Serves 4

Minty grapefruit cups

METRIC/IMPERIAL/AMERICAN
3 large, thin-skinned grapefruit
2 large oranges
175 g/6 oz/1¼ cups seedless white grapes
50 g/2 oz/½ cup almonds, blanched, shredded and toasted
mint sprigs to garnish
MINT DRESSING:
2 teaspoons lemon juice
2 tablespoons/2 tablespoons/3 tablespoons oil
1 tablespoon castor sugar
2 teaspoons finely chopped fresh mint
salt and freshly ground pepper

Halve the grapefruit. Scoop out the flesh all together with a grapefruit knife. Cut out segments with a sharp knife over a bowl to reserve the juice. Cut all peel and pith from the oranges, and cut into segments, discarding the membrane. Mix together the grapefruit, orange, grapes and almonds.

Shake all the ingredients for the dressing together in a screw-topped jar, adding a little of the grapefruit juice. Add to the fruits and toss. Spoon into the grapefruit shells and chill until ready to serve. Garnish with mint sprigs.
Note: When seedless grapes are unavailable, use whole grapes, halved and depipped.

Serves 6

Pineapple japonaise basket

METRIC/IMPERIAL/AMERICAN
1 large pineapple
2 large oranges
225 g/8 oz/½ lb tomatoes, skinned, quartered and deseeded
juice of 1 lemon
1 teaspoon castor sugar
chopped walnuts to garnish
TARRAGON DRESSING:
1 large egg
3 tablespoons/3 tablespoons/¼ cup tarragon vinegar
2 tablespoons/2 tablespoons/3 tablespoons castor sugar
150 ml/¼ pint/⅔ cup double cream, whipped

Cut the pineapple in half lengthwise. Remove the flesh carefully with a grapefruit knife without damaging the shells. Reserve the shells. Remove the pineapple core and cut the flesh into cubes. Cut away all skin and pith from the oranges. Remove the segments, discarding the membrane. Mix with the pineapple. Cut the tomatoes into strips and add with the lemon juice and sugar. Chill.

Beat the egg in a bowl, add the vinegar and sugar and stir continuously over a pan of boiling water until thick. Leave to cool completely before folding in the cream. Adjust seasoning. Spoon the drained pineapple mixture into the reserved shells. Sprinkle with chopped walnuts. Serve with the tarragon dressing and cocktail biscuits.

Serves 6

Fish dishes

The following fish recipes can be either served as a fish course after the starter, or as the main course. If you are serving a fish course the quantities need only be small, just enough to tempt the appetite.

When buying fish you must always check that it is really fresh. The flesh must be firm and not flabby, the eyes and any natural markings should be bright.

If you are lucky enough to acquire a salmon trout when they are in season, try serving it hot, with a dill and cucumber sauce.

A fish fondue can be a huge success at a dinner party – everyone is involved in cooking the food at the table. It is also ideal for the hostess as all the preparation can be done in advance, leaving her completely free to enjoy the company of her guests.

Stuffed plaice florentine

METRIC/IMPERIAL/AMERICAN
$\frac{3}{4}$–1 kg/1$\frac{1}{2}$–2 lb/1$\frac{1}{2}$–2 lb fresh spinach, cooked
1 small onion, finely chopped
25 g/1 oz/2 tablespoons butter
2 egg yolks
freshly grated nutmeg
4 large whole fillets of plaice, skinned and trimmed
100 ml/4 fl oz/$\frac{1}{2}$ cup white wine
juice of 1 lemon
25 g/1 oz/2 tablespoons butter
25 g/1 oz/$\frac{1}{4}$ cup plain flour
300 ml/$\frac{1}{2}$ pint/1$\frac{1}{4}$ cups milk
$\frac{1}{2}$ teaspoon French mustard
75 g/3 oz/$\frac{3}{4}$ cup Cheddar cheese, grated
pinch cayenne pepper
2 tablespoons/2 tablespoons/3 tablespoons cream

Chop spinach. Sauté onion in butter, then add spinach and cook for 5 minutes. Add yolks, nutmeg, salt and pepper. Cool.

Divide the spinach mixture between the plaice fillets and roll up from tail to head. Place in a greased ovenproof dish. Pour over the wine and lemon juice and cover. Bake in a moderate oven (180°C, 350°F, Gas Mark 4) for 20 minutes.

Melt the butter, add the flour and stir for 1 minute. Add the milk and bring to the boil. Stir in the mustard, most of the cheese, fish juices, cayenne, salt, pepper and cream; heat gently. Coat fillets with sauce, sprinkle with cheese and brown.

Serves 4

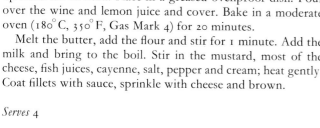

Sole fourée

METRIC/IMPERIAL/AMERICAN
4 whole Dover soles, skinned on both sides
1 small onion, finely chopped
40 g/1½ oz/3 tablespoons butter
100 g/4 oz/1 cup button mushrooms, quartered
20 g/¾ oz/3 tablespoons plain flour
150 ml/¼ pint/⅔ cup each milk and single cream
grated rind of ½ lemon
100 g/4 oz/⅔ cup peeled prawns
1 teaspoon chopped parsley
100 g/4 oz/2 cups fresh white breadcrumbs
50 g/2 oz/¼ cup butter, melted
slices of lemon, watercress and parsley to garnish

Cut along the backbone of each fish between the head and tail. Scrape back the flesh on both sides to each edge to expose the bone. Turn over and repeat on the other side. Using scissors, cut away the backbone, keeping the whole shape of the fish. Cut off the heads. Place in a buttered ovenproof dish.

Prepare the filling by sautéeing the onion in the butter. Add the mushrooms and sauté for 2 minutes. Stir in the flour and cook for 1 minute before adding the milk and cream. Bring to the boil for 2 minutes. Add the lemon rind, prawns, parsley, salt and pepper. Cool. Spoon the filling into the sole 'pockets' and sprinkle with breadcrumbs. Spoon over the melted butter and bake in a moderate oven (180°C, 350°F, Gas Mark 4) for 20–30 minutes, basting well. Lift on to a serving dish and garnish.

Serves 4

Danish halibut steaks

METRIC/IMPERIAL/AMERICAN
salt and pepper
4 halibut steaks
200 ml/8 fl oz/1 cup white wine
juice of 1 lemon
350 g/12 oz/¾ lb fresh asparagus, trimmed, or 1 (283-g/10-oz/10-oz) can asparagus spears, drained
175 g/6 oz/1½ cups button mushrooms, thinly sliced
40 g/1½ oz/3 tablespoons butter
25 g/1 oz/¼ cup plain flour
175 ml/6 fl oz/¾ cup milk
150 ml/¼ pint/⅔ cup single cream
1 tablespoon chopped parsley
twists of lemon to garnish

Season the fish and place in a buttered ovenproof dish. Pour over the wine and half the lemon juice. Cover with butter papers or foil and poach in a moderate oven (180°C, 350°F, Gas Mark 4) for 15–20 minutes until the steaks are just cooked. Keep warm. Meanwhile, cook the fresh asparagus. Trim the asparagus tips and keep warm. Cut the remainder into pieces.

Sauté the mushrooms in the remaining lemon juice for 2–3 minutes. Melt the butter, stir in the flour and cook for 1 minute. Add the milk and fish juices and bring to the boil for 2 minutes. Add the cream, asparagus pieces and mushrooms. Season and add parsley. Lift the halibut on to a serving dish with the asparagus and cover with sauce. Garnish.

Serves 4

Fish kebabs

METRIC/IMPERIAL/AMERICAN
MARINADE:

1 onion, very finely chopped
1 large clove garlic, crushed
150 ml/$\frac{1}{4}$ pint/$\frac{2}{3}$ cup oil
100 ml/4 fl oz/$\frac{1}{2}$ cup white wine
grated rind and juice of 1 lemon
1 heaped tablespoon chopped parsley
1 teaspoon chopped fennel

1 kg/2 lb/2 lb halibut steak or other firm white fish,
   skinned and boned
225 g/8 oz/$\frac{1}{2}$ lb small onions, blanched and quartered
350 g/12 oz/$\frac{3}{4}$ lb tomatoes, skinned and thickly sliced
bay leaves

To make the marinade, sauté the onion and garlic gently in the
oil. Add the remaining ingredients, season to taste and cool. Cut
the halibut into 2.5–4-cm/1–1$\frac{1}{2}$-inch cubes. Place in the
marinade with the onions. Cover and leave for at least 2–3 hours
in a cool place.

Arrange the marinated fish on kebab skewers, alternating
with the onions, tomatoes and bay leaves. Place on a grill pan.
Spoon over any extra marinade and grill for 7–10 minutes on
each side until the fish is cooked through and golden brown.
Serve on a bed of hot cooked rice with any cooking juices
poured over. Serve with an orange sauce, if liked.

Serves 4–6

Trout Belinda

METRIC/IMPERIAL/AMERICAN

1 medium onion, finely chopped
175 g/6 oz/1$\frac{1}{2}$ cups mushrooms, chopped
50 g/2 oz/$\frac{1}{4}$ cup butter
1 (225-g/8-oz/$\frac{1}{2}$-lb) packet frozen leaf spinach, cooked
1 tablespoon chopped fresh herbs
grated rind of $\frac{1}{2}$ lemon
pinch grated nutmeg
6 rainbow trout, boned
seasoned flour
150–175 g/5–6 oz/$\frac{3}{4}$ cup butter
2 large lemons
pinch sugar
100 ml/4 fl oz/$\frac{1}{2}$ cup white wine
2 teaspoons chopped parsley

Prepare a stuffing by sautéeing the onion and mushrooms in
melted butter. Add the chopped spinach, herbs, lemon rind and
nutmeg; then season to taste. Pipe or spoon this mixture
carefully into the trout. Toss the fish in seasoned flour and fry
slowly in half the butter until browned on both sides.

Cut the lemons into thin slices, reserving any juice. Fry the
lemon slices on both sides in the remaining butter with a little
sugar. Place on the trout. Add the white wine and any juice
from the lemons to the pan. Boil until reduced. Add parsley and
pour over the trout.

Serves 6

Salmon trout with dill and cucumber sauce

METRIC/IMPERIAL/AMERICAN
½ bottle white wine
1 medium onion, finely chopped
1 bay leaf
juice of 1 lemon
6 peppercorns
1.25–1.5 kg/2½–3 lb/2½–3 lb whole salmon trout
75 g/3 oz/6 tablespoons butter, melted
DILL AND CUCUMBER SAUCE:
4 egg yolks
1 teaspoon chopped dill
175 g/6 oz/¾ cup soft butter
juice of 1 small lemon
150 ml/¼ pint/⅔ cup double cream, whipped
½ cucumber, peeled and finely chopped
1 teaspoon chopped parsley

Heat the wine, 600 ml/1 pint/2½ cups water, onion, bay leaf, lemon juice and peppercorns in a fish kettle. Simmer for 15 minutes. Add the whole fish and simmer gently for 35–40 minutes without boiling. Drain the fish, remove skin and lift on to a serving dish. Garnish, pour butter over trout and hand sauce separately.

Cream yolks with salt and pepper, dill and a little butter until thick. Add lemon juice and whisk in a bowl over hot water over a gentle heat until thick. Still whisking, add butter. Fold in cream, cucumber and parsley.

Serves 6

Salmon Louise

METRIC/IMPERIAL/AMERICAN
4 salmon steaks
150 ml/¼ pint/⅔ cup white wine
juice of 1 lemon
1 slice onion
6 peppercorns
watercress sprigs to garnish
TOMATO SAUCE:
1 bunch spring onions, shredded
25 g/1 oz/2 tablespoons butter
½ cucumber, peeled, cut into coarse matchsticks,
    blanched and drained
225 g/8 oz/½ lb tomatoes, skinned and quartered
salt and pepper
chopped parsley

Poach the steaks in the wine with lemon juice, onion and peppercorns added, in a covered dish in a moderate oven (180°C, 350°F, Gas Mark 4) for about 15 minutes, depending on the thickness of the fish, until just cooked. Carefully remove the skin from the salmon.

Meanwhile, prepare the sauce. Sauté the spring onions in melted butter. Add the cucumber sticks and sauté quickly. Stir in the tomatoes and heat through carefully. Season, adding a little parsley.

Spoon the tomato sauce into a dish and place salmon on top. Spoon over tarragon-flavoured hollandaise sauce and garnish.

Serves 4

Fish fondue with sauces

METRIC/IMPERIAL/AMERICAN
225 g/8 oz/½ lb haddock or cod fillet, cooked
40 g/1½ oz/3 tablespoons butter
40 g/1½ oz/6 tablespoons plain flour
150 ml/¼ pint/⅔ cup milk
3 tablespoons/3 tablespoons/¼ cup double cream
lemon juice
salt and cayenne pepper
whitebait, washed
whole prawns
whole button mushrooms, washed

For the fish balls, mix the fish with a white sauce (see page 19), adding curry paste if liked. Add lemon juice and seasoning to taste and beat well. Chill. Form into walnut-sized balls with floured hands and then coat with egg and breadcrumbs.

Place a few fish balls, whitebait, prawns and mushrooms on individual plates for each guest to spear and cook in the fondue pan. Serve with rice, salad and sauces.

Avocado sauce: Mash a ripe avocado pear with lemon juice and French dressing. Add a little mayonnaise, double cream, Worcestershire sauce, diced cucumber and seasoning.

Tomato chilli sauce: Mix together mayonnaise, tomato chutney, finely grated onion, 1–2 teaspoons Tabasco, lemon juice, salt and pepper, and whipped cream.

Serves 4

Mediterranean fish casserole

METRIC/IMPERIAL/AMERICAN
450 g/1 lb/1 lb cod steak, skinned and cut into cubes
450 g/1 lb/1 lb halibut, skinned and cut into cubes
seasoned flour
6 tablespoons/6 tablespoons/½ cup oil
350 g/12 oz/¾ lb onions, peeled, halved and sliced
3 cloves garlic, crushed
350 g/12 oz/¾ lb tomatoes, skinned and quartered
1 teaspoon tomato purée
½ bottle dry white wine
juice of 1 lemon
pinch thyme
½ teaspoon fennel
1 tablespoon chopped parsley
generous litre/1 quart/5 cups mussels, prepared (see page 12)
900 ml/1½ pints/3 cups whole prawns
chopped parsley to garnish

Toss the cubed cod and halibut in seasoned flour. Heat 3–4 tablespoons oil and fry the cubes until browned. Remove. Add remaining oil to the pan and sauté the onions and garlic. Add the tomatoes, tomato purée, white wine, lemon juice and herbs and bring to the boil. Return the fish cubes to the pan and simmer gently, covered, for 10–15 minutes until just cooked. Add the mussels, cover and leave for 3–4 minutes until they open. Discard any that do not open. Add the prawns. Sprinkle with parsley.

Serves 6

Meat dishes

The recipes in this section have all been created to form the main part of the meal, probably the most exciting course on the menu. You can really go to town with these recipes, remembering that the final presentation is very important.

For those that like traditional dishes there is Beef Wellington or a Crown roast, or the more adventurous hostess may like to serve a Carré de porc à l'orange. In fact there is something for every taste, whether it be beef, lamb, pork, veal or offal. Remember to choose suitable vegetables to complement the particular meat you are serving.

Beef Wellington

METRIC/IMPERIAL/AMERICAN

1.25 kg/2½ lb/2½ lb whole fillet of beef (thick end)
2 tablespoons/2 tablespoons/3 tablespoons brandy
1 clove garlic, cut in half
50 g/2 oz/¼ cup butter
225 g/8 oz/2 cups onions, finely chopped
225 g/8 oz/2 cups mushrooms, finely chopped
1 teaspoon chopped parsley
3 slices cooked ham, cut in half
1 (368-g/13-oz/13-oz) packet frozen puff pastry, thawed
beaten egg to glaze

Trim the fillet and marinate in brandy for a few hours. Rub with cut garlic and season with pepper. Melt the butter and brown the fillet all over. Pour over the brandy marinade and ignite, then cool. Add the onions and mushrooms to the pan and fry until soft. Season, add the parsley and cool. Mark the fillet into 6 portions and cut two-thirds through. Fold the ham slices in half and sandwich between the cuts.

Roll the pastry to a rectangle double the size of the fillet. Spread the mushroom mixture over. Lay the fillet on top, cut side down. Fold over the pastry to make a parcel, sealing with water. Lift on to a greaseproof covered baking sheet with the folds underneath and brush with egg. Lightly score the pastry. Use trimmings to make pastry leaves. Bake in a hot oven (230°C, 450°F, Gas Mark 8) for 30–40 minutes until browned. Garnish with watercress and serve with Béarnaise sauce.

Serves 6

Beef maçonnaise

METRIC/IMPERIAL/AMERICAN
MARINADE:
½ bottle red wine
1 onion, thinly sliced
1 clove garlic, crushed
1 carrot, thinly sliced
salt and coarsely ground pepper

1.5 kg/3 lb/3 lb topside of beef, cubed
2 tablespoons/2 tablespoons/3 tablespoons oil
225 g/8 oz/½ lb onions, sliced
1 clove garlic, crushed
1 (396-g/14-oz/14-oz) can tomatoes
150 ml/¼ pint/⅔ cup stock
1 bay leaf
225 g/8 oz/2 cups button mushrooms, trimmed
50–75 g/2–3 oz/½ cup black olives, stoned

Boil marinade ingredients, leave until cold then pour over the meat. Next day, drain the meat and keep the marinade. Heat the oil and brown the meat. Transfer to a casserole. Fry the onion and garlic until soft before adding the tomatoes, stock and marinade. Bring to the boil, add the bay leaf and seasoning and pour over the meat. Cover and cook in a moderate oven (180°C, 350°F, Gas Mark 4) for 1½–2 hours. Add the mushrooms 30 minutes before cooking is completed. If liked, cream equal quantities of butter and flour, whisk in sufficient to thicken the sauce. Add the olives and sprinkle with parsley.

Serves 6

Crown of lamb with apricots

METRIC/IMPERIAL/AMERICAN
2 (6–7 bone) best ends neck of lamb
salt and freshly ground pepper
2 tablespoons/2 tablespoons/3 tablespoons oil
mustard and cress to garnish
SAUCE:
25 g/1 oz/¼ cup cornflour
50 g/2 oz/¼ cup soft brown sugar
3 tablespoons/3 tablespoons/¼ cup vinegar
450 ml/¾ pint/2 cups red wine and water mixed
1 tablespoon tomato ketchup
450 g/1 lb/1 lb fresh apricots, halved and stoned

Ask your butcher to form the best ends of lamb into a crown. Season and place in a roasting tin. Brush well with oil and cover bone tips with a strip of foil to prevent charring. Roast in a moderately hot oven (200°C, 400°F, Gas Mark 6) for 1¼–1½ hours, basting during cooking.

Meanwhile, blend the cornflour and sugar with the vinegar. Bring the wine and water and tomato ketchup to the boil, add the cornflour mixture, stir well and bring to the boil, stirring. Add the apricot halves and simmer for 10 minutes until just cooked but still whole.

Remove the foil from the crown. Lift on to a serving dish. Fill the centre of the crown with most of the apricots and moisten with a little sauce. Surround with remaining apricots and sauce. Place a cutlet frill on each bone and garnish.

Serves 6

Noisettes d'agneau Arlésienne

METRIC/IMPERIAL/AMERICAN
0.75 g/1½ lb/1½ lb joint of best end neck of lamb
salt and freshly ground pepper
1 tablespoon chopped fresh herbs
2 cloves garlic, halved
1 aubergine, cut into 4–5-cm/1½–2-inch cubes
2 tablespoons/2 tablespoons/3 tablespoons oil
225 g/8 oz/½ lb onions, halved and thickly sliced
225 g/8 oz/½ lb tomatoes, skinned and quartered
pinch basil
chopped parsley
50 g/2 oz/¼ cup butter

Bone the lamb. Dust with seasoning and herbs and roll up. Secure with string at 2-cm/¾-inch intervals. Cut between the string into noisettes. Rub garlic over and reserve.

Sprinkle the aubergine with salt and leave for 30 minutes. Rinse, drain and dry the aubergine cubes and quickly brown in the oil in a deep frying pan. Remove from the pan. Fry the onions with reserved garlic cloves, crushed, in the same pan. Return aubergines to pan with tomatoes, basil and some parsley. Season and simmer, covered, for 10 minutes.

Heat butter and sauté noisettes for 5–8 minutes each side. Remove string and arrange on a dish with the vegetables. Sprinkle with parsley and place a pat of savoury butter on each.

Serves 4–6

Veal escalopes italienne

METRIC/IMPERIAL/AMERICAN
50 g/2 oz/¼ cup butter
4 escalopes of veal, beaten flat
2 red peppers, halved, cored, sliced and blanched
1 clove garlic, crushed
175–225 g/6–8 oz/2 cups button mushrooms, sliced
200 ml/8 fl oz/1 cup Marsala
150 ml/¼ pint/⅔ cup stock
lemon juice

Melt the butter in a large deep frying pan and fry the seasoned escalopes briskly for 5–7 minutes on each side until well browned. Remove and fry the peppers and garlic for 2 minutes. Add the mushrooms and fry until just soft. Add Marsala and ignite; then stir in the stock and bring to the boil. Replace the escalopes, season, cover the pan and simmer for 10–12 minutes. Place the escalopes on a serving dish, adding lemon juice to taste. Spoon the sauce over.

Variation: Veal viennoise   *Illustrated on the cover*

Dip the escalopes in seasoned flour, brush with beaten egg and coat with an equal mixture of dry white breadcrumbs and grated Parmesan cheese. Fry in melted butter for 7–10 minutes on each side. Add a little lemon juice. Garnish with anchovy fillets, chopped or sieved egg yolk and chopped egg white (see picture). Surround with cooked asparagus, sliced lemon, tomato and watercress.

Serves 4

Pork stroganoff

METRIC/IMPERIAL/AMERICAN
50 g/2 oz/¼ cup butter
1 small onion, chopped
175 g/6 oz/1½ cups button mushrooms, trimmed
1 teaspoon French mustard
1 teaspoon tomato purée
150 ml/¼ pint/⅔ cup soured cream
1 tablespoon oil
0.75–1 kg/1½–2 lb/1½–2 lb pork fillet, cut into thin strips
100 ml/4 fl oz/½ cup vermouth
pinch dried basil and tarragon
juice of ½ lemon
salt and freshly ground pepper
GARNISH:
chopped parsley
lemon wedges

Melt half the butter in a pan and slowly fry the onion and mushrooms until soft. Add the mustard, tomato purée and most of the soured cream then set aside. Heat the oil and remaining butter together and fry the meat over a high heat until well browned. Pour over the vermouth and ignite. Blend in the sauce, adding herbs, lemon juice and seasoning to taste. Simmer gently for 10 minutes, stirring occasionally. Serve with a little soured cream spooned over. Sprinkle with parsley and garnish with lemon wedges. Serve with rice.

Serves 4–6

Carré de porc à l'orange

METRIC/IMPERIAL/AMERICAN
2 small (6 bone) best ends of pork, skinned
1 onion, finely chopped
2 sticks celery, finely chopped
25 g/1 oz/2 tablespoons butter
100 g/4 oz/ 2 cups fresh white breadcrumbs
grated rind and juice of 1 orange
50 g/2 oz/⅓ cup raisins
2 teaspoons chopped parsley
50 g/2 oz/¼ cup soft brown sugar
juice of 1 orange and ½ lemon
1 tablespoon Worcestershire sauce
150 ml/¼ pint/⅔ cup each white wine and stock
2 oranges, sliced and fried in butter to garnish

Ask the butcher to trim the cutlets and make into a guard of honour. Fry the onion and celery in the butter. Add to the breadcrumbs, orange rind, raisins, parsley, salt and pepper and mix well. Bind with the orange juice. Place this stuffing in the middle of the guard of honour in a roasting tin. Bring the sugar, orange and lemon juices and Worcestershire sauce to the boil. Spoon over the meat and roast in a moderately hot oven (190°C, 375°F, Gas Mark 5) for about 2 hours, basting regularly.

Top bones with cutlet frills and place on a serving dish. Remove fat from the juices in the tin then add the wine and stock. Bring to the boil, season and serve with the pork. Arrange fried orange slices around the meat.

Serves 6

Chinese spare ribs

METRIC/IMPERIAL/AMERICAN
1 kg/2 lb/2 lb spare ribs of pork
3 tablespoons/3 tablespoons/$\frac{1}{4}$ cup tomato ketchup
4 tablespoons/4 tablespoons/$\frac{1}{3}$ cup clear honey
4 tablespoons/4 tablespoons/$\frac{1}{3}$ cup soy sauce
2 cloves garlic, crushed
6 tablespoons/6 tablespoons/$\frac{1}{2}$ cup wine vinegar
1 tablespoon tomato purée
3 tablespoons/3 tablespoons/$\frac{1}{4}$ cup sherry
salt and pepper

Trim any excess fat from the spare ribs and cut down between
the ribs into pieces. Mix all the remaining ingredients together
and use to marinate the pork for at least 6 hours and preferably
overnight, in a strong polythene bag or plastic container. Shake
well occasionally to mix the marinade thoroughly. Place the ribs
with the marinade in a roasting tin and cook in a moderately hot
oven (200°C, 400°F, Gas Mark 6) for 1 hour. Drain off the
liquid and leave the ribs to cook until crisp.

Meanwhile, remove the fat from the cooking liquid and boil
over a high heat until reduced to a syrup. Place the spare ribs in
a serving dish and spoon the sauce over.
Note: This makes a very good informal supper dish served with
rice and a Chinese salad (see page 42). Also popular as a
barbecue party dish.

Serves 4–6

Ham Véronique

METRIC/IMPERIAL/AMERICAN
1–1.25 kg/2–2$\frac{1}{2}$ lb/2–2$\frac{1}{2}$ lb corner or slipper of bacon
few slices root vegetables for flavouring
2 bay leaves
6 peppercorns
200 ml/8 fl oz/1 cup white wine
1 onion, finely chopped
50 g/2 oz/$\frac{1}{4}$ cup butter
40 g/1$\frac{1}{2}$ oz/6 tablespoons plain flour
300 ml/$\frac{1}{2}$ pint/1$\frac{1}{4}$ cups veal or chicken stock
salt and pepper
2 egg yolks
150 ml/$\frac{1}{4}$ pint/$\frac{2}{3}$ cup cream
225 g/8 oz/$\frac{1}{2}$ lb white grapes, peeled and depipped
chopped parsley

Simmer the bacon in a saucepan with water to cover and with
the vegetables, bay leaves and peppercorns; allow 20 minutes
per 0.5 kg/1 lb plus 15 minutes over. Cool.

Boil the wine with the onion until reduced by half. Melt the
butter, add the flour and cook for a few minutes. Add the stock,
bring to the boil and add the strained white wine. Season. Pour
a little sauce on to the yolks and cream mixed. Whisk back into
the pan and reheat without boiling. Add the grapes. Drain the
ham, strip off the skin and slice. Arrange on a dish with some of
the sauce. Sprinkle with parsley and serve the remaining sauce
separately.

Serves 6

Spicy gammon steaks

METRIC/IMPERIAL/AMERICAN
2 teaspoons dry mustard
2 teaspoons powdered cinnamon
100 g/4 oz/½ cup soft brown sugar
4 gammon steaks, 1-cm/½-inch thick
juice of 2 large oranges
1 (454-g/16-oz/16-oz) can peach halves
450 g/1 lb/1 lb cooking apples, peeled, quartered, cored
    and sliced
2 tablespoons/2 tablespoons/3 tablespoons chutney
20 g/¾ oz/3 tablespoons cornflour
watercress sprig to garnish

Mix the mustard, cinnamon and sugar together and spoon half
the mixture over the gammon steaks, arranged in an ovenproof
dish. Make the orange juice up to 450 ml/¾ pint/2 cups with the
juice from the drained peaches and pour round the gammon.
Cover with foil and bake in a moderate oven (180°C, 350°F, Gas
Mark 4) for 45 minutes. Arrange the apples over the steaks and
spoon over the remaining spicy mixture. Baste with juices and
return to the oven, uncovered, for a further 30 minutes. Spoon
chutney into the peach halves, place in an ovenproof dish and
heat through in the oven for 10 minutes. Serve with the
gammon.
   Place the gammon steaks on a dish. Thicken the juices with
the cornflour blended with a little water. Spoon over the steaks
and garnish.

Serves 4

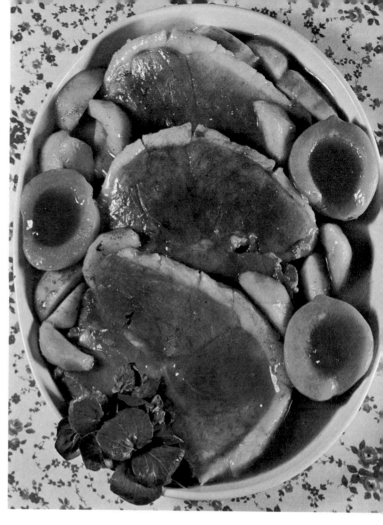

Lambs' kidneys bourguignonne

METRIC/IMPERIAL/AMERICAN
50 g/2 oz/¼ cup butter
8 lambs' kidneys, skinned, halved and cored
200 ml/8 fl oz/1 cup red wine
225 g/8 oz/½ lb button onions, peeled and blanched
1 clove garlic, crushed
225 g/8 oz/2 cups whole button mushrooms, trimmed
45 g/1¾ oz/scant ½ cup plain flour
300 ml/½ pint/1¼ cups stock
1 bay leaf
salt and freshly ground pepper
225 g/8 oz/½ lb tomatoes, skinned, quartered and
    deseeded
chopped parsley to garnish

Melt half the butter in a pan and sauté the kidneys quickly over a
high heat until browned. Add the wine and ignite. Transfer to a
casserole. Melt the remaining butter in the pan and lightly
brown the onions and garlic, add the mushrooms and fry for a
further 2–3 minutes. Add to the casserole. Stir the flour into the
pan juices then gradually add the stock and bring to the boil for
2 minutes. Add to the kidneys in the casserole with the bay leaf
and seasoning. Cover and simmer gently for 20–25 minutes.
Add the tomatoes and continue to cook for 5 minutes. Discard
bay leaf and garnish. Serve with saffron rice, if liked.

Serves 4–6

Sweetbreads Florentine

METRIC/IMPERIAL/AMERICAN

0.75 kg/1½ lb/1½ lb calves' sweetbreads, soaked in salted
   water overnight
75 g/3 oz/6 tablespoons butter
1 onion, finely chopped
1 clove garlic, crushed
100 ml/4 fl oz/½ cup white wine
1 bay leaf
450 g/1 lb/1 lb cooked leaf spinach
grated nutmeg
75 g/3 oz/¾ cup cheese, grated
300 ml/½ pint/1¼ cups béchamel sauce (see page 12)
cayenne pepper

Drain the sweetbreads. Cover with water and bring to boil.
Refresh with cold water, trim and press between 2 plates. Melt
half the butter, add onion, garlic and sweetbreads and sauté for
10 minutes. Add wine, bay leaf, salt and pepper; simmer for
about 10 minutes.

   Meanwhile, toss the spinach in the remaining butter, adding
nutmeg, salt and pepper. Arrange in a hot serving dish. Add 50 g/
2 oz/½ cup cheese to the béchamel sauce (see page 12), together
with 150 ml/¼ pint/⅔ cup cooking liquor from the sweetbreads
and salt and cayenne. Simmer gently. Place the sweetbreads in
the centre of the spinach and cover with sauce. Sprinkle with
cheese and brown in the top of a moderately hot oven (200°C,
400°F, Gas Mark 6) for about 10 minutes.

Serves 4

Cotelettes de veau Foyot

METRIC/IMPERIAL/AMERICAN

4 best end neck of veal cutlets, trimmed
salt and freshly ground pepper
50–75 g/2–3 oz/4–6 tablespoons butter
225 g/8 oz/2 cups onions, chopped
1 clove garlic, crushed
1 tablespoon chopped parsley
40 g/1½ oz/¾ cup fresh white breadcrumbs
50 g/2 oz/½ cup Parmesan cheese, freshly grated
pinch cayenne pepper
300 ml/½ pint/1¼ cups white wine and veal or chicken
   stock mixed

Season the cutlets and brown on each side in 50 g/2 oz/¼ cup of
the butter. Remove. Add the onions and garlic to the pan and
fry gently until lightly coloured. Remove from the heat, add the
parsley and spoon half the mixture into a deep ovenproof dish.
Arrange the cutlets on top. Add the breadcrumbs and cheese to
the remaining onion mixture. Mix well, season, adding cayenne,
and press on top of each cutlet. Melt the remaining butter and
spoon over the topping on the cutlets. Add the wine and stock
to the pan, heat and pour round the cutlets. Cover with a lid or
foil and cook in a moderate oven (160°C, 325°F, Gas Mark 3)
for 45 minutes, basting occasionally. Remove the foil and cook
for a further 30 minutes until the meat is tender and topping
brown.

Serves 4

Poultry and game dishes

For those special dinner and supper parties, here are some exotic recipes for poultry and game. Poultry is always readily available but game is restricted to certain times of the year. If you are looking for an excuse to have a dinner party, have one when game is in season! Serve pheasant cooked in Calvados and wine or with chestnuts, partridge cooked with onions and mushrooms in red wine, barbecued duck and many more delicious dishes.

Included in this section is a recipe for Chicken parisienne. This is an unusual way of serving chicken as the bird is boned and then stuffed. It makes a very attractive dish and easy to serve at the table.

Poussin à l'estragon

METRIC/IMPERIAL/AMERICAN
1 lemon
handful fresh tarragon or 1 tablespoon dried tarragon
3 (0.75-kg/1½–2-lb/1½–2-lb) baby chickens, prepared
175 g/6 oz/¾ cup butter
200 ml/8 fl oz/1 cup white wine
225 g/8 oz/2 cups onions, finely chopped
225 g/8 oz/2 cups button mushrooms, sliced
40 g/1½ oz/6 tablespoons plain flour
300 ml/½ pint/1¼ cups stock
1 tablespoon chopped parsley
watercress sprigs to garnish

Squeeze the lemon juice. Remove leaves from fresh tarragon. Cut up lemon skin and put a piece inside each bird with the tarragon stalks and a knob of butter. Keep 50 g/2 oz/¼ cup of butter and spread the remainder over chickens. Put in a roasting tin, pour over wine and cook in a moderate oven (180°C, 350°F, Gas Mark 4) for 40–50 minutes.

Sauté the onions in the reserved butter, add the mushrooms and sauté. Sprinkle on the flour and cook for 1 minute. Add the stock, bring to boil and add reserved lemon juice, chopped tarragon, parsley, salt and pepper. Simmer for 15 minutes.

When the chickens are cooked, strain the juices into the sauce and cook to a coating consistency. Just before serving, cut each bird in half with poultry scissors. Arrange chicken in a dish. Spoon over sauce, serve with mushrooms and garnish.

Serves 6

31

Chicken parisienne

METRIC/IMPERIAL/AMERICAN

1 (1.5-kg/3½-lb/3½-lb) roasting chicken, prepared
50 g/2 oz/¼ cup soft butter
150 ml/¼ pint/⅔ cup stock
3 tablespoons/3 tablespoons/¼ cup sherry
watercress to garnish

STUFFING:

1 onion, finely chopped
25 g/1 oz/2 tablespoons butter
225 g/8 oz/1 cup each veal and ham, minced
3 tablespoons/3 tablespoons/¼ cup fresh white
    breadcrumbs
2 teaspoons chopped parsley
1 teaspoon chopped tarragon
grated rind and juice of ½ lemon
1 egg, beaten

Bone the chicken, taking care not to puncture the skin. Spread out skin side downwards on a board and season.

For the stuffing, sauté the onion in the butter. Cool and mix with the minced meats, breadcrumbs, herbs and lemon rind. Bind together with egg and lemon juice, season. Spread over the chicken and sew up.

Spread 50 g/2 oz/¼ cup butter over chicken, place in a roasting tin with stock and sherry. Cook in a moderately hot oven (190°C, 375°F, Gas Mark 5) for 1½ hours, basting well. Slice chicken and serve, if liked, with a mushroom sauce.

Serves 4–6

Poulet aux amandes

METRIC/IMPERIAL/AMERICAN

100 g/4 oz/½ cup butter
1 (1.5-kg/3½-lb/3½-lb) roasting chicken, prepared
sprig tarragon
150 ml/¼ pint/⅔ cup white wine or chicken stock
50 g/2 oz/½ cup almonds, blanched and shredded
225 g/8 oz/½ lb red peppers, halved and sliced
1 onion, chopped
20 g/¾ oz/3 tablespoons plain flour
300 ml/½ pint/1¼ cups stock
pinch mace
150 ml/¼ pint/⅔ cup single cream
parsley to garnish

Put 15 g/½ oz/1 tablespoon butter inside the bird with the tarragon. Spread 40 g/1½ oz/3 tablespoons butter over the bird and roast with the wine in a moderately hot oven (200°C, 400°F, Gas Mark 6) for about 1 hour, basting well.

Melt the remaining butter and fry the almonds until brown. Add the peppers and onion and sauté until soft. Remove. Add the flour to the pan and cook for 1 minute, then add the stock, mace, salt and pepper. Return the almond and pepper mixture with the strained juices from the cooked chicken. Bring back to the boil and add the cream.

To serve, joint the chicken and arrange on a dish. Spoon over the sauce and garnish.

Serves 4–6

Poulet au citron

METRIC/IMPERIAL/AMERICAN

2 tablespoons/2 tablespoons/3 tablespoons oil
50 g/2 oz/¼ cup butter
1 (1.5-kg/3½-lb/3½-lb) roasting chicken, jointed
1 onion, finely chopped
1 clove garlic, crushed
¼ teaspoon powdered saffron
200 ml/8 fl oz/1 cup white wine
300 ml/½ pint/1¼ cups chicken stock
pared rind and juice of 1 lemon
175 g/6 oz/1½ cups button mushrooms, quartered
25 g/1 oz/¼ cup plain flour
2 egg yolks and 150 ml/¼ pint/⅔ cup single cream

Heat the oil in a pan. Add 25 g/1 oz/2 tablespoons butter and brown the chicken pieces. Remove to an ovenproof casserole. Add the onion and garlic to the pan and when softened add the saffron, wine and stock. Bring to the boil, adding lemon juice, salt and pepper and pour over the chicken. Cover and simmer for 45–60 minutes. Cut lemon rind into fine strips, blanch and add most of the strips to the chicken at end of cooking.

For the sauce, melt the remaining butter and sauté the mushrooms. Sprinkle on the flour and cook for 1 minute. When the chicken is cooked, pour the cooking juices into the mushroom mixture. Pour some of this on to the yolks and cream mixed and return to pan. Reheat gently without boiling. Spoon over chicken on a dish. Sprinkle with lemon strips.

Serves 4

Pheasant Vallée d'Auge

METRIC/IMPERIAL/AMERICAN

1 tablespoon oil
50 g/2 oz/¼ cup butter
1 plump pheasant, prepared
100 ml/4 fl oz/½ cup Calvados
1 onion, thinly sliced
2 sticks celery, thinly sliced
225 g/8 oz/2 cups Cox's apples, peeled and sliced
15 g/½ oz/2 tablespoons plain flour
100 ml/4 fl oz/½ cup white wine
300 ml/½ pint/1¼ cups chicken stock
salt and freshly ground pepper
150 ml/¼ pint/⅔ cup double cream
apple rings and watercress to garnish

Heat the oil in a frying pan, add 25 g/1 oz/2 tablespoons butter and brown the pheasant. Add the Calvados and ignite. Place the pheasant in a casserole. Add the remaining butter to the pan and sauté the onion for 5 minutes. Add the celery and apple, cook for 5 minutes then stir in the flour, wine and stock. Bring to the boil, season and pour over the pheasant. Cover and simmer for 45–50 minutes.

To serve, lift the pheasant on to a serving dish and keep warm. Remove the fat from the pan juices then liquidise or sieve. Place in a pan and bring to the boil. Whisk in the cream and cook until thickening. Adjust seasoning and serve with the pheasant separately. Garnish and serve.

Serves 4–6

Pheasant casserole with chestnuts

METRIC/IMPERIAL/AMERICAN
1 tablespoon oil
25 g/1 oz/2 tablespoons butter
1 plump pheasant, prepared
225 g/8 oz/½ lb button onions, skinned
225 g/8 oz/½ lb fresh chestnuts, peeled and skinned
25 g/1 oz/¼ cup plain flour
450 ml/¾ pint/2 cups stock
100 ml/4 fl oz/½ cup red wine
grated rind and juice of 1 orange
2 teaspoons redcurrant jelly
1 bay leaf
salt and freshly ground pepper
chopped parsley to garnish

Heat the oil in a frying pan, add the butter and brown the pheasant all over. Cut into serving pieces and place in a casserole. Add the onions and chestnuts to the pan and cook until golden brown, then transfer to the casserole. Add the flour to the frying pan and cook for 1 minute before whisking in the stock, wine, orange rind and juice and redcurrant jelly. Bring to the boil, add the bay leaf and season to taste. Pour over the pheasant, cover and cook in a moderate oven (160°C, 325°F, Gas Mark 3) for 1½–2 hours until tender. Remove the bay leaf and any fat from the juices. Adjust seasoning and garnish.

Serves 4–6

Partridge bourguignonne

METRIC/IMPERIAL/AMERICAN
50 g/2 oz/¼ cup butter
2 partridges, prepared
175 g/6 oz/6 oz lean bacon, cut in strips and blanched
150 ml/¼ pint/⅔ cup red wine
300 ml/½ pint/1¼ cups chicken stock
1 teaspoon tomato purée
bouquet garni
salt and freshly ground pepper
350 g/12 oz/¾ lb pickling onions, skinned
1 clove garlic, crushed
175 g/6 oz/1½ cups button mushrooms
1 tablespoon chopped parsley

Melt 25 g/1 oz/2 tablespoons butter in a pan and brown the birds. Transfer to a casserole. Brown the bacon in the same pan, add the wine, stock and tomato purée. Bring to the boil. Pour into the casserole adding bouquet garni and seasoning. Cover and cook in a moderate oven (180°C, 350°F, Gas Mark 4) for 1 hour.

Meanwhile, melt the remaining butter in a pan, add the onions and garlic and brown. Add the mushrooms. Add with parsley to casserole 30 minutes before end of cooking time.

To serve, cut each bird in half with poultry scissors. Remove backbone, trim wing and leg bones and place in a deep serving dish. Remove the bouquet garni from the sauce, adjust seasoning and spoon over.

Serves 4

Salmis of grouse

METRIC/IMPERIAL/AMERICAN
2 older grouse, cut into pieces
350 g/12 oz/¾ lb lean pie pork, cut into 5-cm/2-inch pieces
100 g/4 oz/¼ lb lean raw gammon, soaked and diced
seasoned flour
50 g/2 oz/¼ cup butter
150 ml/¼ pint/⅔ cup red wine
bouquet garni
2 sprigs fresh tarragon or 1 teaspoon dried tarragon
¼ teaspoon mixed spice
900 ml/1½ pints/3¾ cups game or chicken stock
coarsely grated rind and juice of 1 orange
salt and freshly ground pepper

Toss the pieces of grouse, pork and gammon in seasoned flour.
Heat the butter in a frying pan and brown the pieces all over.
Transfer to a flameproof casserole. Flame the wine, if liked, and
add to the casserole with the bouquet garni, tarragon, mixed
spice, stock and orange juice. Bring to the boil, season, cover
the casserole and cook in a moderate oven (160°C, 325°F, Gas
Mark 3) for 1½–2 hours until tender.

Spoon the pieces of meat into a serving dish. Remove and
discard the bouquet garni, and boil the sauce until reduced to a
syrupy consistency. Pour over the meats, sprinkle with grated
orange rind before serving.

Serves 4–6

Pigeons forestière

METRIC/IMPERIAL/AMERICAN
1 tablespoon oil
25 g/1 oz/2 tablespoons butter
2–4 pigeons, depending on size, prepared
175 g/6 oz/6 oz chipolata sausages, twisted in half
1 (175-g/6-oz/6-oz) piece of bacon, cut into strips
1 onion, finely chopped
150 ml/¼ pint/⅔ cup dry sherry
300 ml/½ pint/1¼ cups stock
bouquet garni
175 g/6 oz/1½ cups button mushrooms, quartered
225 g/8 oz/½ lb button onions, blanched and browned
25 g/1 oz/2 tablespoons soft butter
25 g/1 oz/¼ cup plain flour
watercress to garnish

Heat the oil, add the butter and brown the pigeons. Remove to
a casserole. Add the sausages and blanched bacon to the pan and
brown. Remove the sausages. Add the onion and soften before
adding the sherry. Pour into the casserole with the stock and
bouquet garni. Bring to the boil, add salt and pepper, cover
tightly and simmer for 35–40 minutes. Add the mushrooms,
onions and sausages and cook for a further 10 minutes.

Cream the butter and flour. Lift out the pigeons and arrange
in a deep serving dish. Remove the bouquet garni then whisk in
small pieces of butter and flour. Bring to the boil and simmer
for 2 minutes. Spoon over the pigeons and garnish.

Serves 4

Duck Montmorency

METRIC/IMPERIAL/AMERICAN
1 (2.25–2.75-kg/5–6-lb/5–6-lb) duckling, prepared
2 oranges
25 g/1 oz/2 tablespoons butter
100 ml/4 fl oz/$\frac{1}{2}$ cup red wine
450 g/1 lb/1 lb dark red cherries, stoned
25–50 g/1–2 oz/2–4 tablespoons sugar
pinch powdered cinnamon
4 tablespoons/4 tablespoons/$\frac{1}{3}$ cup redcurrant jelly
150 ml/$\frac{1}{4}$ pint/$\frac{2}{3}$ cup port or red wine
15 g/$\frac{1}{2}$ oz/2 tablespoons arrowroot
watercress to garnish

Prick the duck all over with a fork. Squeeze the juice from 1 orange and place the skins and the butter inside the bird. Place the duck in a roasting tin and pour over the orange juice and wine. Roast in a moderately hot oven (200°C, 400°F, Gas Mark 6) for 1–1$\frac{1}{2}$ hours. Turn the duck over halfway through cooking time, strain off any excess fat. Put the cherries and any juice with the sugar and cinnamon into an ovenproof dish. Cover and cook in the bottom of the oven for 10 minutes. Cool. Boil the redcurrant jelly and port with the grated rind and juice of remaining orange. Add the cherries and thicken with arrowroot and water mixed.

To serve, cut the duck into 4 portions. Spoon the fat off the pan juices, add the juices to the cherry sauce and bring to the boil. Spoon over the duck and garnish.

Serves 4

Barbecued duck

METRIC/IMPERIAL/AMERICAN
1 (2.25–2.75-kg/5–6-lb/5–6-lb) duckling, prepared
1 teaspoon dry mustard
$\frac{1}{4}$ teaspoon each cayenne and pepper
2 oranges
1 clove garlic, crushed
$\frac{1}{4}$ teaspoon Tabasco sauce
2 tablespoons/2 tablespoons/3 tablespoons Worcestershire sauce
2 tablespoons/2 tablespoons/3 tablespoons tomato purée
4 tablespoons/4 tablespoons/$\frac{1}{3}$ cup red wine
2 tablespoons/2 tablespoons/3 tablespoons lemon juice
2 teaspoons paprika
1 teaspoon soft brown sugar
flaked almonds, orange twists and watercress to garnish

Prick the duck all over with a fork. Mix together the mustard, cayenne and pepper and rub into the bird. Place breast down in a dry roasting tin in a hot oven (220°C, 425°F, Gas Mark 7) for 20 minutes. Meanwhile, thinly pare the rind from the oranges, shred finely and blanch. Squeeze the orange juice and mix with the pared rind and remaining ingredients, season. Strain the fat off the duck and turn the bird over. Pour the mixture over and roast for about 1$\frac{1}{4}$ hours at 180°C, 350°F, Gas Mark 4, basting.

When cooked, cut the duck into serving joints and return to the drained roasting dish to crisp in the oven. Arrange the duck on a serving dish and spoon over the sauce. Garnish.

Serves 4

Vegetable dishes and salads

Vegetables and salads do not always get the attention and credit they deserve. They not only add colour and texture to the meal but also provide valuable nutrients to the diet. With this book as your guide, you can create some interesting combinations of vegetable and salad ideas, such as new potatoes with cucumber.

There are also many unusual salads that will make a refreshing accompaniment to any meal.

Braised celery with walnuts

METRIC/IMPERIAL/AMERICAN
1 head celery, trimmed and washed
salt and freshly ground pepper
1 medium onion, finely chopped
50 g/2 oz/¼ cup butter
50 g/2 oz/½ cup broken shelled walnuts
coarsely grated rind of 1 lemon

Cut the celery into 4-cm/1½-inch slanting sticks. Blanch in boiling salted water for 5 minutes. Sauté the onion in 25 g/ 1 oz/2 tablespoons butter then add the celery and sauté gently for 5–10 minutes until tender but still crisp. Meanwhile, fry the walnuts in the remaining butter for 1–2 minutes until crisp. Stir in the lemon rind then add to the celery and toss well. Season to taste.

Serves 4

Cauliflower amandine

METRIC/IMPERIAL/AMERICAN
1 medium cauliflower
salt and freshly ground pepper
75 g/3 oz/6 tablespoons butter
100 g/4 oz/1 cup whole almonds, blanched and shredded
chopped parsley to garnish

Break the cauliflower into florets then trim, wash and cook in boiling salted water for 10–15 minutes until just cooked but still crisp. Drain. Melt the butter and sauté the almonds until golden brown. Toss gently with the cauliflower and season to taste. Turn into a serving dish and sprinkle with parsley.

Serves 4

Spinach italienne

METRIC/IMPERIAL/AMERICAN
1 kg/2 lb/2 lb fresh leaf spinach, thoroughly washed and
   shredded
2 tablespoons/2 tablespoons/3 tablespoons oil
75 g/3 oz/6 tablespoons butter
1 clove garlic, roughly chopped
100 g/4 oz/¼ lb back bacon, cut into thin strips
100 g/4 oz/¼ lb Italian salami, cut into thin strips
salt and freshly ground pepper
pinch nutmeg
lemon juice

Blanch the spinach in boiling salted water for 3–5 minutes until tender but not too soft. Drain thoroughly. Heat the oil in a frying pan. Add 50 g/2 oz/¼ cup of the butter and sauté the garlic until brown. Remove and discard. Add the bacon and salami and sauté until crisp. Add the drained spinach and remaining butter. Reheat thoroughly and season to taste, adding nutmeg to bring out the flavour of the spinach and a little lemon juice. Turn into a serving dish.

Serves 4

Fantail potatoes

METRIC/IMPERIAL/AMERICAN
6 medium potatoes, peeled and shaped into even-sized
 ovals
1 slice lemon
50 g/2 oz/¼ cup butter
1 onion, finely chopped
salt and freshly ground pepper
25 g/1 oz/¼ cup Parmesan cheese, grated
25 g/1 oz/¼ cup Cheddar cheese, grated
parsley sprig to garnish

Cut each potato into thin vertical slices but leaving a hinge at
the base. Soak in cold water with a slice of lemon added, until all
are completed. Melt the butter in a pan and fry the onion until
soft. Drain the potatoes and arrange cut side upwards in an
ovenproof dish. Spoon the onion and butter over and season.
Cook at the top of a moderately hot oven (190°C, 375°F, Gas
Mark 5) for 30 minutes, basting occasionally. Mix the cheeses
and sprinkle over the potatoes. Continue cooking for a further
20–30 minutes until crisp and golden brown.

Serves 6

Minty new potatoes with cucumber

METRIC/IMPERIAL/AMERICAN
450 g/1 lb/1 lb small new potatoes, washed and scraped
few mint stems
salt and pepper
½ large cucumber, peeled
50 g/2 oz/¼ cup butter
2 teaspoons chopped fresh mint
150 ml/¼ pint/⅔ cup single cream (optional)

Cook the potatoes with mint stems in boiling salted water for
10–15 minutes until just tender. Quarter the cucumber
lengthwise and cut across into cubes. Melt the butter in a pan
and sauté the cucumber for 5 minutes. Add the drained cooked
potatoes and chopped mint. Season to taste and toss thoroughly. Add the cream, if used, and heat to just below boiling. Turn
into a serving dish.

Serves 4–6

Devilled mushrooms

METRIC/IMPERIAL/AMERICAN
4 slices white bread, 2.5 cm/1 inch/1 inch thick
oil for frying
1 clove garlic, chopped
350 g/12 oz/3 cups button mushrooms, trimmed
25 g/1 oz/2 tablespoons butter
juice of ½ lemon
150 ml/¼ pint/⅔ cup double cream, whipped
1 tablespoon tomato ketchup
1 tablespoon horseradish sauce
1 tablespoon Worcestershire sauce
1 teaspoon French mustard
few drops Tabasco sauce
grated nutmeg
salt and pepper
parsley sprigs to garnish

Cut the bread into four 10-cm/4-inch diameter circles. Cut out a 7.5-cm/3-inch diameter circle almost to the bottom and remove the centre carefully to form a case. Fry gently in shallow oil with the garlic, on both sides until crisp. Drain on kitchen paper.

Meanwhile, sauté the mushrooms quickly in the butter for 1 minute. Remove from the heat, add the lemon juice and spoon into the bread cases. Mix the cream with the remaining ingredients. Season and spoon over the mushrooms. Cook at the top of a hot oven (220°C, 425°F, Gas Mark 7) for 5–10 minutes. Garnish.

Serves 4

Citron salad

METRIC/IMPERIAL/AMERICAN
1 small head celery, washed and trimmed
2 large oranges
225 g/8 oz/½ lb chicory, washed and trimmed
juice of 1 lemon
1 bunch watercress, washed and picked into sprigs
DRESSING:
1 teaspoon French mustard
1 tablespoon sugar
salt and freshly ground pepper
150 ml/¼ pint/⅔ cup single cream
3 tablespoons/3 tablespoons/¼ cup oil
1 tablespoon white wine vinegar

Cut the celery into 6.5-cm/2½-inch lengths and shred into very fine matchsticks. Soak in iced water for at least 1 hour until curled.

Grate the rind of half an orange for the dressing. Cut away peel and pith from both oranges and remove the segments from between the membranes with a sharp knife. Place in a bowl with any juice. Make up the dressing by placing the mustard, sugar, seasoning, cream, oil and vinegar in a screw-topped jar with the orange rind and juices. Shake well together.

Cut the chicory into diagonal slices and toss with lemon juice. Add celery curls, orange segments and most of the watercress. Arrange in a salad bowl with remaining watercress. Toss with the dressing.

Serves 4

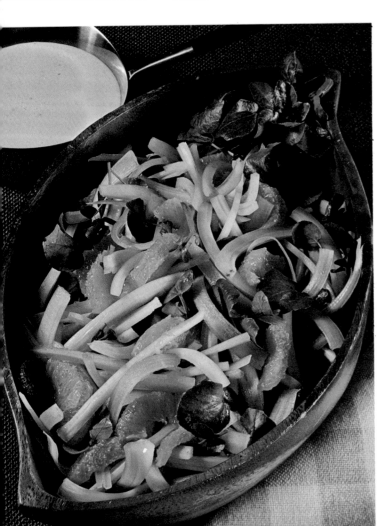

Caesar salad

METRIC/IMPERIAL/AMERICAN
FRENCH DRESSING:
150 ml/¼ pint/⅔ cup olive oil
2 tablespoons/2 tablespoons/3 tablespoons wine vinegar
1 clove garlic, crushed
pinch sugar
salt and freshly ground pepper

175 g/6 oz/1½ cups button mushrooms, thickly sliced
25 g/1 oz/2 tablespoons butter
1 clove garlic, crushed
2 slices white bread, cut into 5-mm/¼-inch/¼-inch cubes
1 cos or Webb's lettuce, well washed and drained
1 ripe avocado pear
juice of ½ lemon
1 teaspoon snipped chives
25 g/1 oz/¼ cup Parmesan cheese, grated

Make up the dressing by shaking oil, vinegar, garlic, sugar and seasoning together in a screw-topped jar. Pour over the mushrooms and leave to marinate for 30 minutes. Melt the butter in a pan with the garlic and sauté the bread cubes until golden brown. Drain on kitchen paper. Tear the lettuce into shreds. Peel, quarter and slice the avocado pear thickly and toss in lemon juice to prevent discoloration. Toss the lettuce and avocado pear together with the mushrooms and dressing. Add the croûtons and pile into a salad bowl. Sprinkle with chives and Parmesan cheese.

Serves 4–6

Mixed salad vinaigrette

METRIC/IMPERIAL/AMERICAN
1 bunch radishes
225 g/8 oz/½ lb courgettes, trimmed
350 g/12 oz/¾ lb tomatoes, quartered and cored
1 red and 1 green pepper, sliced
25–50 g/1–2 oz/⅓ cup black olives or stuffed olives
few crisp lettuce leaves
FRESH HERB DRESSING:
2 tablespoons/2 tablespoons/3 tablespoons wine vinegar
150 ml/¼ pint/⅔ cup olive oil
1 clove garlic
1 teaspoon French mustard
1 shallot, finely chopped
½ teaspoon each basil, tarragon, chervil, chives or spring
    onion tops and parsley, finely chopped
salt and freshly ground pepper

Trim the radishes and cut down with a sharp pointed knife to make flower petals. Leave in iced water in the refrigerator for at least 2 hours.

Cook the courgettes in boiling salted water for 7–10 minutes until just tender. Refresh in cold water. Slice and mix with the tomatoes, peppers, olives and drained radishes. Put all dressing ingredients into a screw-topped jar and shake together with seasoning to taste. Toss into the salad. Pile into a bowl lined with the washed lettuce leaves.

Serves 6

Chinese salad

METRIC/IMPERIAL/AMERICAN

½ cucumber, peeled
225 g/8 oz/4 cups beansprouts, washed and drained
2 red peppers, halved, deseeded and finely sliced
1 (198-g/7-oz/8-oz) can sweetcorn, drained
2 teaspoons chopped parsley
LEMON DRESSING:
2 tablespoons/2 tablespoons/3 tablespoons lemon juice
4 tablespoons/4 tablespoons/⅓ cup olive oil
2 tablespoons/2 tablespoons/3 tablespoons soy sauce
2 tablespoons/2 tablespoons/3 tablespoons single cream
salt and freshly ground pepper
sugar to taste

chopped parsley to garnish

Wipe the cucumber and cut into matchsticks. Mix with the beansprouts, peppers, sweetcorn and parsley. Put all the dressing ingredients into a screw-topped jar and shake well with seasoning and sugar to taste. Add the dressing to the salad and toss well. Serve piled into individual bowls with a little extra parsley sprinkled over. The rind from the lemon may be grated and sprinkled on top, if liked.
Note: Suitable to serve with cold meats and any sweet and sour dishes.

Serves 4–6

Fruit slaw

METRIC/IMPERIAL/AMERICAN

½ medium white cabbage, trimmed, halved and cored
3 tablespoons/3 tablespoons/¼ cup oil
salt and freshly ground pepper
2 Cox's apples, quartered and cored
juice of 1 lemon
225 g/8 oz/½ lb mixed black and white grapes, halved and seeded
½ cucumber, peeled and cut into matchsticks
½ endive, thoroughly washed and drained (optional)
DRESSING:
150 ml/¼ pint/⅔ cup soured cream
2 tablespoons/2 tablespoons/3 tablespoons lemon juice
1 tablespoon castor sugar
salt and pepper
1 tablespoon chopped parsley

Slice the cabbage finely on a mandoline slicer or with a sharp knife. Mix with the oil and seasoning and leave in the refrigerator for 2 hours to soften.

Slice the apples thinly and toss in lemon juice. Add the grapes and cucumber. Mix the dressing ingredients together and add to the salad together with the cabbage. Toss thoroughly. Tear the endive into pieces, if used, and mix into the salad. Spoon the fruit slaw into a salad bowl and serve.

Serves 6

Hot and cold sweets

Care must be taken when selecting a sweet, bearing in mind what has been served previously.

Hot sweets must be timed very carefully, so they are ready when you are! If you have the courage of your convictions, the Grand Marnier soufflé is a must. It will really impress your guests.

The cold sweets have the advantage that they can be made in advance. The summer fruits come into their own in this section. A favourite is the old-fashioned Summer gâteau, sometimes known as a Summer pudding. If you have a freezer it is a good idea to freeze fruit when there is an abundance so that you can enjoy fruits throughout the year.

Grand Marnier soufflé

METRIC/IMPERIAL/AMERICAN
icing sugar or castor sugar
1 packet sponge finger biscuits or sponge cake
6 tablespoons/6 tablespoons/½ cup Grand Marnier
150 ml/¼ pint/⅔ cup milk
75 g/3 oz/6 tablespoons castor sugar
finely grated rind of ½ lemon
thinly pared rind of 1 orange
25 g/1 oz/2 tablespoons butter
25 g/1 oz/¼ cup plain flour
3 eggs, separated

Grease a soufflé dish and dust with the sugar. Line it with the sponge fingers soaked in one-third of the liqueur. Bring the milk, sugar, lemon and orange rinds to the boil over gentle heat. Set aside for 10 minutes. Melt the butter in a large pan. Add the flour and cook for 1 minute before adding the strained milk. Bring slowly to the boil, beating continuously until smooth. Leave to cool, then beat in the egg yolks, one at a time. Add the remaining liqueur.

Whisk the egg whites until stiff but not dry. Stir 1 tablespoon into the soufflé mixture and cut and fold in the rest. Turn into the soufflé dish and smooth the top. Bake in a moderate oven (180°C, 350°F, Gas Mark 4) for 40–45 minutes. Carefully open the door and draw the oven shelf forward. Dust the top of the soufflé with icing sugar then continue cooking for a few minutes to colour. Serve at once.

Serves 4–6

Summer gâteau

METRIC/IMPERIAL/AMERICAN

3 eggs
95 g/3¾ oz/bare ½ cup castor sugar
grated rind of ½ lemon
75 g/3 oz/¾ cup plain flour, sifted with ½ teaspoon ground cinnamon and a pinch of salt
1–1.25 kg/2–2½ lb/2–2½ lb mixed soft fruits as available – redcurrants, blackcurrants, raspberries, loganberries, strawberries (sliced), blackberries
soft brown sugar
50 g/2 oz/½ cup split almonds, toasted
300 ml/½ pint/1¼ cups double cream, whipped
sugar to taste

Whisk the eggs, sugar and lemon rind in a bowl over hot water until thick. Remove from the heat and whisk until cold. Fold in the sifted flour and spread the mixture evenly into a Swiss roll tin lined with greased greaseproof paper. Bake in a moderate oven (180°C, 350°F, Gas Mark 4) for 15–20 minutes until cooked. Leave to cool. Turn out and cut the sponge to line a 1.25-litre/2-pint/2½-pint basin, reserving enough for a lid.

Reserve some whole fruit for decoration then mix the remaining fruits for filling with soft brown sugar to taste. Add the almonds and pack into the basin right to the top. Press down well and cover with the sponge lid. Weight down and chill for 24 hours. Turn out. Sweeten cream. Pipe rosettes over the sponge. Decorate with reserved fruit.

Serves 6

Stuffed pears with Cointreau and orange sauce

METRIC/IMPERIAL/AMERICAN

200 g/7 oz/scant 1 cup sugar
450 ml/¾ pint/2 cups water
thinly pared rind of 2 oranges, shredded and blanched
juice of 2 oranges
6 William pears
1–2 tablespoons Cointreau
FILLING:
75 g/3 oz/¾ cup ground almonds
50 g/2 oz/½ cup icing sugar
25 g/1 oz/2 tablespoons butter, softened
grated rind and juice of 1 lemon and 1 orange

Bring the sugar, water and orange shreds to the boil and cook for 5 minutes until a syrup forms. Add orange juice.

Mix together the almonds, sugar, butter and lemon and orange rinds. Bind with a little orange juice if necessary. Peel the pears, leaving them whole, then remove core from the base. Dip in lemon juice and fill with the almond mixture. Stand in an ovenproof dish and pour the syrup over with any remaining orange and lemon juice. Cover and bake in a moderate oven (180°C, 350°F, Gas Mark 4) for 20–25 minutes until tender. Baste with syrup during cooking. Remove the pears to a serving dish and keep warm. Boil the syrup until reduced. Add liqueur and spoon over pears.

Serves 6

Apricot and almond strudel

METRIC/IMPERIAL/AMERICAN
1 packet strudel pastry (2 sheets)
melted butter
450 g/1 lb/1 lb fresh apricots, stoned and sliced
100 g/4 oz/1 cup ground almonds
25 g/1 oz/¼ cup flaked almonds
grated rind of 1 lemon
75 g/3 oz/6 tablespoons castor sugar

Spread one sheet of pastry on a tea towel and brush with melted butter. Place the second sheet on top and brush again. Mix the apricots, almonds, lemon rind and sugar together and spoon over the pastry. Roll up with the help of the tea towel, folding in the ends. Cover a baking sheet with non-stick paper and lift on the strudel, forming into a horseshoe shape. Bake in a moderately hot oven (200°C, 400°F, Gas Mark 6) for 30 minutes until crisp and golden brown. Slide on to a serving dish and dust with icing sugar. Serve hot or cold with cremet.

To make cremet, pour 300 ml/½ pint/1¼ cups milk into a pan, reserving about 2 tablespoons. Bring gently to the boil. Meanwhile, mix 2 heaped teaspoons custard powder with sugar to taste and the reserved milk. Remove the boiled milk from the heat, stir in the custard and return to the heat to thicken, stirring. Leave to cool. Add 150 ml/5 fl oz/⅔ cup natural yogurt and chill before serving.

Serves 4–6

Normandy apple pie

METRIC/IMPERIAL/AMERICAN
2 egg yolks
100 g/4 oz/½ cup castor sugar
40 g/1½ oz/3 tablespoons butter
50 g/2 oz/¼ cup lard
2 tablespoons/2 tablespoons/3 tablespoons water
225 g/8 oz/2 cups plain flour, sifted
¾ teaspoon powdered cinnamon
50 g/2 oz/½ cup walnuts, finely ground
0.5–0.75 kg/1–1½ lb/1–1½ lb Cox's apples, peeled, cored and quartered
150 ml/¼ pint/⅔ cup double cream, lightly whipped
Calvados or brandy (optional)

Cream together the egg yolks, sugar, butter, lard and water. Add the flour, cinnamon and walnuts gradually and work together to a paste. Knead until smooth. Wrap and chill in the refrigerator for at least 30 minutes. Roll out two-thirds of the pastry and use to line a 20-cm/8-inch fluted flan ring. Arrange the prepared apples, cut side down, in the flan case. Roll out the remaining pastry to make a lid. Dampen the edges, position and press together. Cut a 7.5-cm/3-inch circle out of the centre of the lid. Brush the pastry with cold water and dust with castor sugar. Bake in a moderate oven (180°C, 350°F, Gas Mark 4) for 35–40 minutes until the pastry is crisp and cooked. Just before serving pipe the whipped cream, flavoured with liqueur and sugar to taste, around the centre.

Serves 6

Raspberry dacquoise

METRIC/IMPERIAL/AMERICAN
175 g/6 oz/1¼ cups whole almonds
7 egg whites
400 g/14 oz/1¾ cups castor sugar
large pinch cream of tartar
0.75 kg/1½ lb/1½ lb raspberries, fresh or frozen
600 ml/1 pint/2½ cups double cream
castor sugar to taste
icing sugar

Blanch the almonds and grind in a mouli grater. Whisk egg whites until stiff. Add 1 tablespoon of measured sugar and whisk for a further 2–3 minutes. Fold in the rest of the sugar with the almonds and cream of tartar. Pipe the mixture into three separate circles on to baking sheets lined with non-stick paper, using a plain 1-cm/½-inch nozzle. Bake in a very cool oven (110°C, 225°F, Gas Mark ¼) for 1–1½ hours until dry. Leave to cool.

Meanwhile, reserve some raspberries for decoration and whip the cream with sugar to taste. Place a meringue circle on a suitable serving dish. Spread one-third of the cream over the base and sprinkle with a few raspberries. Repeat the layers and press the remaining meringue on top. Dust with icing sugar, pipe rosettes of cream around the edge and decorate with the remaining whole raspberries.
Note: This gâteau must not be assembled more than 1–1½ hours before serving or it will become too soft.

Serves 6

Chocolate and orange roulade

METRIC/IMPERIAL/AMERICAN
5 eggs, separated
175 g/6 oz/¾ cup castor sugar
175 g/6 oz/6 squares plain chocolate, melted to a cream
    with 2 tablespoons/2 tablespoons/3 tablespoons water
6 large oranges
450 ml/¾ pint/2 cups double cream

Whisk the egg whites until stiff. In a separate bowl, whisk the egg yolks and sugar until thick and very pale in colour. Add the melted chocolate then fold in the whisked egg whites. Spread evenly in a Swiss roll tin lined with non-stick paper. Bake in a moderate oven (180°C, 350°F, Gas Mark 4) for 20–25 minutes until cooked. Cover with a layer of wet kitchen paper. Wrap in cling film and leave overnight. Carefully turn out on to greaseproof paper well dusted with icing sugar and peel off non-stick paper.

For the filling, finely grate the rind of 1 orange. Cut away peel and pith from all the oranges with a sharp knife and remove the segments over a bowl to catch the juice. Whip the cream with the orange rind and any juice until thick. Add sugar to taste. Reserving some cream for decoration, spread the remainder over the sponge. Keep some orange segments for decoration and scatter the rest along the middle of the sponge. Roll up and turn on to a flat serving dish. Dust with icing sugar. Pipe stars of cream on top, decorate with orange segments and chill.

Serves 6

Galette noisette Normande

METRIC/IMPERIAL/AMERICAN
75 g/3 oz/6 tablespoons butter
65 g/2½ oz/5 tablespoons castor sugar
125 g/4½ oz/1 cup plus 2 tablespoons plain flour, sifted
　　with a pinch of salt
75 g/3 oz/⅔ cup hazel nuts, toasted and ground
0.75 kg/1½ lb/1½ lb Cox's apples, peeled and cored
3 cloves
grated rind and juice of 1 lemon
1 tablespoon smooth apricot jam
50 g/2 oz/⅓ cup sultanas or raisins
300 ml/½ pint/1¼ cups double cream
icing sugar and toasted hazel nuts to decorate

Beat together butter and sugar. Add flour and nuts and knead
until smooth. Wrap and chill for at least 30 minutes.

Slice the apples and cook with the cloves, lemon rind, juice
and jam over low heat until soft. Remove the cloves. Add the
sultanas and cook for 5 minutes longer. Leave to cool.

Divide the pastry into three. Roll into 20-cm/8-inch circles
on non-stick paper. Place on baking sheets. Bake in a moderate
oven (180°C, 350°F, Gas Mark 4) for 15–20 minutes. While still
warm cut one round into six portions. Whip the cream and
reserve some for decoration. Spread half of the remainder on
one pastry round and cover with half the apple mixture. Repeat
the layers and place cut portions on top. Dust with icing sugar.
Pipe a rosette of cream on to each portion and decorate.

Serves 6

Gâteau Paris Brest

METRIC/IMPERIAL/AMERICAN
150 ml/¼ pint/⅔ cup water
50 g/2 oz/¼ cup butter
65 g/2½ oz/½ cup plus 2 tablespoons plain flour, sifted
　　twice with a pinch of salt
2 eggs, lightly whisked
25 g/1 oz/¼ cup flaked almonds
little castor sugar
2 egg whites, stiffly whisked
450 ml/¾ pint/2 cups double cream, whipped
450 g/1 lb/1 lb strawberries, tossed in sugar

Prepare the choux paste by heating the water and butter slowly
until the butter has melted. Bring to the boil, draw aside and
immediately add all the flour. Beat until the mixture becomes
smooth and leaves the sides of the pan. Leave to cool before
beating in the eggs gradually and thoroughly until smooth and
shiny. Using a plain 2.5-cm/1-inch nozzle, pipe on to a greased
baking sheet in a 23-cm/9-inch ring. Sprinkle with almonds and
dust with sugar. Bake in a moderately hot oven (200°C, 400°F,
Gas Mark 6) for 30 minutes. Lower to 180°C, 350°F, Gas Mark
4 and continue until crisp and golden. Remove and cool.

Split the choux ring in half. Fold the egg whites into the
cream and place in a piping bag. Use two-thirds to fill the base
ring then cover with the strawberries and pipe the rest of the
cream on top. Lightly press the almond-covered ring on top,
dust with icing sugar and serve.

Serves 6

Vacherin Chantilly glacé

METRIC/IMPERIAL/AMERICAN
100 g/4 oz/½ cup granulated sugar
pared rind and juice of 1 medium lemon
225 g/8 oz/½ lb strawberries, fresh or frozen
50 g/2 oz/½ cup icing sugar
juice of 1 large orange
6 egg whites
275 g/10 oz/1¼ cups castor sugar
whipped cream and fresh strawberries to decorate

For the sorbet: simmer sugar, 300 ml/½ pint/1¼ cups water and lemon rind for 5 minutes. Cool and strain. Liquidise the strawberries with the icing sugar, sieve and add the orange and lemon juices and sugar syrup. Freeze in a shallow container. When half-frozen, beat well. Whisk one egg white until stiff and fold in. Freeze until hard.

For the meringue case, whisk the remaining egg whites until stiff. Add 50 g/2 oz/¼ cup of the measured sugar and whisk hard for 3½ minutes. Fold in the remaining sugar. Reserve a quarter of the meringue in the refrigerator and, using a large star nozzle, pipe about two-thirds of the remainder into a 20-cm/8-inch circle on a baking sheet lined with non-stick paper. Pipe the remaining one-third into a second wide border round the edge of the circle. Cook in a very cool oven (110°C, 225°F, Gas Mark ¼) until slightly coloured. Pipe the reserved meringue on top of the second border while the case is still hot. Return to the oven to dry. When cool, pile sorbet into meringue case; decorate.

Serves 6

Bavaroise française

METRIC/IMPERIAL/AMERICAN
pared rind and juice of 1 lemon
300 ml/½ pint/1¼ cups milk
4 egg yolks
50 g/2 oz/¼ cup castor sugar
15 g/½-oz packet/1 envelope powdered gelatine soaked in 3 tablespoons/3 tablespoons/¼ cup cold water
300 ml/½ pint/1¼ cups double cream, whipped
2 egg whites, whisked
450 g/1 lb/1 lb fresh black cherries
3 tablespoons/3 tablespoons/¼ cup redcurrant jelly

Add the lemon rind to the milk and bring to the boil slowly over a gentle heat. Infuse for 10 minutes. Beat the egg yolks and sugar together until thick. Pour on the milk and return to the rinsed pan. Thicken the custard over a very gentle heat, stirring continously. Add the soaked gelatine, remove from the heat and stir until the gelatine is dissolved. Strain into a bowl and cool. When the mixture begins to thicken, fold in two-thirds of the cream and then the egg whites and pour into a wetted savarin mould. Chill until set.

Stone the cherries, reserving any juice. Melt the redcurrant jelly with the lemon juice in a pan and add any cherry juice. Cool then add the cherries.

Turn out the bavaroise ring on to a serving dish. Pile some of the prepared cherries in the centre. Decorate with rosettes of the reserved cream and the remaining cherries around the edge.

Serves 6

Charlotte mexicaine

METRIC/IMPERIAL/AMERICAN
225 g/8 oz/8 squares plain chocolate, coarsely grated
450 ml/¾ pint/2 cups strong coffee
3 eggs, separated
50 g/2 oz/¼ cup castor sugar
15 g/½-oz packet/1 envelope powdered gelatine, soaked in
    3 tablespoons/3 tablespoons/¼ cup cold water
300 ml/½ pint/1¼ cups double cream, lightly whipped
300 ml/½ pint/1¼ cups double cream, thickly whipped
langue de chat biscuits
coarsely grated chocolate

Dissolve the chocolate in the coffee. Cream the egg yolks and sugar until thick and pale in colour. Add the chocolate mixture. Return to the rinsed pan and thicken over a gentle heat, without boiling, stirring continuously. Remove the pan from the heat, add the soaked gelatine to the custard and stir until dissolved. Strain into a bowl and cool. Add the lightly whipped cream. Whisk the egg whites until stiff and fold into the mixture. When on the point of setting, pour into a lightly oiled straight-sided 18-cm/7-inch mould or cake tin with a removable base. Leave in the refrigerator to set.

To serve, turn out and spread a thin layer of whipped cream round the sides. Press the biscuits around. Put the remaining cream into a piping bag and pipe small stars down each biscuit join. Decorate the top with rosettes of thickly whipped cream and grated chocolate.

Serves 6

Strawberry mille feuille

METRIC/IMPERIAL/AMERICAN
350 g/12 oz/¾ lb puff pastry
600 ml/1 pint/2½ cups double cream
sugar to taste
3 tablespoons/3 tablespoons/¼ cup orange liqueur
1 kg/2 lb/2 lb medium strawberries, hulled
icing sugar

Divide the pastry into three. Roll each piece into a strip approximately 13 x 30 cm/5 x 12 inches. Trim the edges evenly with a sharp knife. Place each strip on a wet baking sheet. Prick all over and bake in a hot oven (220°C, 425°F, Gas Mark 7) for 10–15 minutes until golden brown and well risen. Leave to cool on a wire rack.

Whisk the cream and flavour with sugar and liqueur. Place one pastry sheet on a flat serving dish. Spread with some of the cream and cover with half the prepared strawberries. Repeat the layers and cover with the remaining pastry. Press down lightly. Dredge with sifted icing sugar.

Serves 6

Pineapple soufflé en surprise

METRIC/IMPERIAL/AMERICAN

4 eggs, separated
100 g/4 oz/½ cup castor sugar
150 ml/¼ pint/⅔ cup canned pineapple juice
15 g/½-oz packet/1 envelope powdered gelatine
2 tablespoons/2 tablespoons/3 tablespoons cold water
juice of 1 large lemon
150 ml/¼ pint/⅔ cup double cream, whipped
1 medium fresh pineapple, peeled, cored and cubed
sugar to taste
Kirsch (optional)
whipped cream and angelica leaves to decorate

Surround a 15–18-cm/6–7-inch soufflé dish with double grease-proof paper and secure firmly with string. Place a small well-oiled jar in the centre.

Whisk the egg yolks, sugar and pineapple juice over hot water until thick. Remove from the heat and continue whisking until cold. Soak the gelatine in the water and dissolve over a gentle heat. Add the lemon juice and stir into the mixture. Fold in the cream then the stiffly whisked egg whites. Pour into the soufflé dish and leave to set. Meanwhile, marinate the pineapple with sugar and Kirsch.

When the soufflé is firm, remove the paper surrounding the dish then gently remove the jam jar from the centre. Fill the hole with the pineapple and decorate the top.

Serves 4–6

Caramel oranges with Cointreau

METRIC/IMPERIAL/AMERICAN

6 large seedless oranges
350 g/12 oz/1½ cups granulated sugar
300 ml/½ pint/1¼ cups water
3 tablespoons/3 tablespoons/¼ cup Cointreau
CARAMEL:
175 g/6 oz/¾ cup granulated sugar
4 tablespoons/4 tablespoons/⅓ cup water

Pare the rind thinly from 4 oranges and cut into long julienne strips. Blanch for 15 minutes. Drain and refresh. Bring the sugar and water to the boil, add the orange strips and simmer for 20 minutes. Add Cointreau and cool.

Cut away all skin and pith from the oranges. Slice each orange thinly and reshape, holding together with a cocktail stick. Strain the syrup over the oranges, reserving the orange strips. Chill thoroughly.

Meanwhile, make the caramel by dissolving the sugar in the water. Cook steadily to a rich brown colour, without stirring. Pour immediately on to a well-oiled surface or waxed paper. Leave to harden, then crush in a mortar or with a rolling pin. Sprinkle over the oranges, together with the reserved strips of rind. Serve with cream handed separately.

Serves 6

Fresh peach and almond flan

METRIC/IMPERIAL/AMERICAN
100 g/4 oz/½ cup butter
75 g/3 oz/6 tablespoons castor sugar
grated rind of ½ lemon
1 small egg
1 egg yolk
175 g/6 oz/1½ cups plain flour, sifted
75 g/3 oz/¾ cup ground almonds
3 large ripe peaches, halved
175 g/6 oz/¾ cup granulated sugar dissolved in 300 ml/
    ½ pint/1¼ cups water
175 g/6 oz/¾ cup cream cheese
grated rind of 1 small lemon
2 tablespoons/2 tablespoons/3 tablespoons single cream
25 g/1 oz/2 tablespoons castor sugar
25 g/1 oz/¼ cup ground almonds
whole blanched almonds and angelica to decorate

For the almond pastry, blend the butter, sugar, lemon rind and
eggs until well mixed. Work in the flour and almonds and knead
to a smooth paste. Wrap and chill for at least 1 hour. Line a flan
ring with the pastry. Bake blind in a moderate oven (180°C,
350°F, Gas Mark 4) for 30 minutes. Leave to cool.
    Poach the peaches in the sugar syrup, then remove the skins.
Reduce the syrup to a glazing consistency. Cool.
    Beat the cream cheese with the lemon rind, cream, sugar and
almonds. Spread over the pastry base. Arrange the peach halves
on top. Brush with syrup glaze and decorate.

Serves 6

Buck's fizz sorbet

METRIC/IMPERIAL/AMERICAN
175 g/6 oz/¾ cup castor sugar
150 ml/¼ pint/⅔ cup water
4 large oranges
finely grated rind and juice of 1 lemon
900 ml/1½ pints/3¾ cups champagne, chilled
2 egg whites, stiffly whisked
2–3 tablespoons/2–3 tablespoons/3–4 tablespoons Grand
    Marnier
50 g/2 oz/2 oz ratafia biscuits
DECORATION:
150 ml/¼ pint/⅔ cup double cream, whipped
orange rind

Bring the sugar and water slowly to the boil. Boil rapidly for
6 minutes to make a syrup. Finely grate the rind of one orange
and add with the lemon rind. Set aside. Cut the remaining
oranges in half lengthwise and scoop out all the flesh. Reserve
the shells. Press the flesh through a nylon sieve into the syrup.
Add the lemon juice and cool. Stir in the champagne and freeze
for 1½–2 hours until frozen round the edges. Whip until smooth
in a mixer or blender. Fold in the egg whites and Grand Marnier
and freeze for at least 3 hours until hard.
    Sit each reserved orange shell in a champagne goblet. Divide
the ratafia biscuits between the shells and sprinkle with Grand
Marnier. Keep chilled until ready to serve. Pile the sorbet into
orange shells. Pipe cream on top, decorate with orange rind.

Serves 6

Egg and cheese dishes

These recipes are particularly suitable to serve at supper parties. Eggs and cheese are two basic ingredients most likely to be kept in stock and the recipes in this section show what versatile and imaginative dishes can be prepared.

A slightly more unusual way of serving a Camembert cheese is shown in the Iced wine Camembert. The cheese is sieved and mixed with wine and butter before it is set and chilled. The Tarte aux oeufs cressonière is to be recommended as the subtle combination of watercress and eggs in a cheese flan case topped with sauce is really mouthwatering.

Smoked salmon quiche

METRIC/IMPERIAL/AMERICAN
PASTRY:
175 g/6 oz/1½ cups plain flour
pinch salt
100 g/4 oz/½ cup butter
1 egg, beaten
FILLING:
3 eggs
300 ml/½ pint/1¼ cups single cream
100–175 g/4–6 oz/4–6 oz smoked salmon, cut into strips
pinch nutmeg
freshly ground pepper
2 teaspoons chopped parsley

To make the pastry, sift the flour and salt into a bowl, then rub in the butter until the mixture resembles breadcrumbs. Bind together with the egg, adding a few drops of cold water if necessary to give a firm dough. Knead lightly, then cover and chill for at least 30 minutes. Roll out and use to line a 20-cm/8-inch flan ring. Prick the base and bake blind in a moderate oven (180°C, 350°F, Gas Mark 4) for 10 minutes.

Beat the eggs with the cream. Add the salmon, nutmeg, pepper to taste and the parsley. Pour into the flan case and return to the oven to cook for 30–35 minutes until set. Serve hot or cold.

Note: Use cheaper ends or off-cuts of smoked salmon.

Serves 4–6

Gruyère roulade

METRIC/IMPERIAL/AMERICAN
40 g/1½ oz/3 tablespoons butter
30 g/1¼ oz/5 tablespoons plain flour
300 ml/½ pint/1¼ cups milk
25 g/1 oz/¼ cup Gruyère cheese, grated
2 tablespoons/2 tablespoons/3 tablespoons cream
350 g/12 oz/¾ lb fresh asparagus, cooked and trimmed
ROULADE:
175 g/6 oz/1½ cups Gruyère cheese, grated
50 g/2 oz/1 cup fresh white breadcrumbs
4 eggs, separated
150 ml/¼ pint/⅔ cup single cream
40 g/1½ oz/6 tablespoons Parmesan cheese, grated

Make a white sauce for the filling with the butter, flour and milk, adding Gruyère cheese, cream and salt and pepper to taste. Warm the asparagus through.

For the roulade, mix the cheese and breadcrumbs together, then work in the egg yolks and cream. Season with salt and cayenne pepper to taste. Whisk the egg whites stiffly and fold into the mixture. Spread the mixture evenly into a Swiss roll tin lined with non-stick paper and sprinkle with a little Parmesan cheese. Bake in a moderately hot oven (200°C, 400°F, Gas Mark 6) for 10–15 minutes until firm. Turn out on to a sheet of greaseproof paper sprinkled with the remaining Parmesan cheese. Spread thickly with the sauce, lay the asparagus along the middle and roll up.

Serves 6

Gougère de la mer

METRIC/IMPERIAL/AMERICAN
CHOUX PASTRY (SEE PAGE 47):
150 ml/¼ pint/⅔ cup water
50 g/2 oz/¼ cup butter
65 g/2½ oz/½ cup plus 2 tablespoons plain flour
2 eggs, beaten
50 g/2 oz/½ cup Gruyère or Cheddar cheese, finely diced
FILLING:
1 onion, finely sliced
50 g/2 oz/½ cup button mushrooms, sliced
25 g/1 oz/2 tablespoons butter
20 g/¾ oz/3 tablespoons plain flour
150 ml/¼ pint/⅔ cup fish stock or milk
2 tablespoons/2 tablespoons/3 tablespoons single cream
350 g/12 oz/2 cups peeled prawns
½ teaspoon each chopped fennel and parsley
25 g/1 oz/¼ cup each Parmesan and browned crumbs
slices of tomato and parsley to garnish

Make up the choux pastry and fold in the cheese. Pipe or spoon the mixture around the sides of a well buttered shallow oven-proof dish, leaving a hollow in the centre. Sauté the onion and mushrooms in the butter, stir in the flour. Add the stock and bring to the boil. Off the heat, add the cream, prawns, herbs and salt and pepper. Spoon into the centre of the dish. Dust with the cheese and breadcrumbs mixed and bake in a moderately hot oven (200°C, 400°F, Gas Mark 6) for 35–40 minutes. Garnish.

Serves 4–6

Egg and spinach ring

METRIC/IMPERIAL/AMERICAN
1.25 kg/2½ lb/2½ lb fresh spinach, cooked and sieved
450 ml/¾ pint/2 cups béchamel sauce (see page 61)
3 eggs
2 tablespoons/2 tablespoons/3 tablespoons cream
350 g/12 oz/¾ lb smoked haddock, cooked and flaked
3 hard-boiled eggs, quartered
pinch cayenne pepper
150 ml/¼ pint/⅔ cup single cream
25 g/1 oz/¼ cup cheese, grated
MORNAY SAUCE (SEE PAGE 55):
20 g/¾ oz/1½ tablespoons butter
20 g/¾ oz/3 tablespoons flour
300 ml/½ pint/1¼ cups milk
50 g/2 oz/½ cup cheese, grated

Heat the spinach gently to dry off. Add the béchamel sauce, then draw aside and beat in the eggs and cream. Season well with salt, pepper and nutmeg. Turn into a well buttered ring mould and cover with buttered paper. Stand in a baking tin with hot water. Bake in a moderate oven (180°C, 350°F, Gas Mark 4) for about 50 minutes until firm.

Make the mornay sauce. Mix the haddock and eggs with half the sauce and season with cayenne. Turn the spinach ring on to a warm ovenproof dish and spoon the filling into the centre. Add the cream to the remaining sauce, heat and spoon over. Sprinkle with cheese and brown under the grill.

Serves 4–6

Pissaladière

METRIC/IMPERIAL/AMERICAN
225 g/8 oz/2 cups plain flour
pinch salt
100 g/4 oz/½ cup butter
50 g/2 oz/¼ cup lard
1 egg yolk
2 tablespoons/2 tablespoons/3 tablespoons cold water
FILLING:
450 g/1 lb/1 lb onions, thinly sliced
3 tablespoons/3 tablespoons/¼ cup oil
2 teaspoons French mustard
350 g/12 oz/¾ lb tomatoes, skinned and thickly sliced
½ teaspoon each chopped basil, thyme and chives
50 g/2 oz/½ cup Gruyère or Cheddar cheese, grated
1 (56-g/2-oz/2-oz) can anchovy fillets
100–175 g/4–6 oz/1 cup black olives, stoned

Make up the pastry (see page 52). Chill then line a 20-cm/8-inch flan dish. Bake blind in a moderately hot oven (200°C, 400°F, Gas Mark 6) for 10 minutes.

Sauté the onions in oil for 20 minutes until golden and season. Spread the mustard over the pastry base. Reserving the oil, drain the onions and spread over the base of the flan. Arrange the tomatoes on top. Sprinkle with herbs and cheese. Arrange halved anchovy strips in a lattice on top and place an olive in each square. Spoon over the oil. Return to the oven for 25–30 minutes.

Serves 4–6

Tarte aux oeufs cressonière

METRIC/IMPERIAL/AMERICAN
175 g/6 oz/1½ cups plain flour
salt and cayenne pepper
100 g/4 oz/½ cup butter
100 g/4 oz/1 cup dry Cheddar cheese, grated
3 bunches watercress, washed and coarsely chopped
20 g/¾ oz/1½ tablespoons butter
1 teaspoon anchovy essence
6 hard-boiled eggs, halved lengthwise
MORNAY SAUCE:
25 g/1 oz/2 tablespoons butter
25 g/1 oz/¼ cup plain flour
300 ml/½ pint/1¼ cups milk
75 g/3 oz/¾ cup Cheddar cheese, grated
½ teaspoon mustard

Sift the flour and seasoning, then rub in the butter. Add the cheese and knead. Cover and chill for 30 minutes. Roll out and line a 20-cm/8-inch flan ring. Bake blind in a moderate oven (180°C, 350°F, Gas Mark 4) for 20–25 minutes.

Meanwhile, sauté the watercress in the butter for 2–3 minutes. Add the essence and season. Melt the butter for the sauce, stir in the flour and cook for 1 minute. Add the milk and bring to the boil. Remove from the heat, stir in two-thirds of the cheese, mustard and seasoning. Spoon the watercress over the flan base. Arrange eggs on top and coat with sauce. Sprinkle with cheese and brown. Garnish with tomato and cress.

Serves 4–6

Egg and Roquefort mousse

METRIC/IMPERIAL/AMERICAN
100 g/4 oz/½ cup Roquefort or Gorgonzola cheese, mashed
½ cucumber, peeled, grated and drained
3 tablespoons/3 tablespoons/¼ cup chopped parsley
½ canned pimento, drained and chopped
1 teaspoon finely chopped onion
15 g/½-oz packet/1 envelope powdered gelatine
3 tablespoons/3 tablespoons/¼ cup lemon juice
300 ml/½ pint/1¼ cups double cream, lightly whipped
salt and pepper
6 hard-boiled eggs, sliced
150 ml/¼ pint/⅔ cup aspic jelly

Mix together the cheese, cucumber, parsley, pimento and onion. Dissolve the gelatine in 150 ml/¼ pint/⅔ cup water, add lemon juice and add to the cheese mixture. Fold in the cream and season. Place a well-oiled straight-sided jar in the centre of a soufflé dish. When the mixture is on the point of setting, spoon a layer into the dish. Cover with a layer of egg slices and repeat the layers until the dish is three-quarters full, ending with a layer of mousse. Make a circle of egg round the edge. Chill. Meanwhile, make up the aspic jelly and cool before spooning over the mousse. Allow to set.

When the mousse is set, run a warm knife round the jar to remove. Fill the centre with tomato and stuffed olives.

Serves 4–6

Iced cheese soufflés

METRIC/IMPERIAL/AMERICAN

75 g/3 oz/¾ cup fresh Parmesan cheese, grated
50 g/2 oz/½ cup Gruyère cheese, grated
½ teaspoon French mustard
salt and pepper
pinch cayenne pepper
300 ml/½ pint/1¼ cups aspic jelly
2 teaspoons tarragon vinegar
100 g/4 oz/½ cup cream cheese
300 ml/½ pint/1¼ cups double cream, whipped
2 egg whites, stiffly whisked
GARNISH:
dry grated Parmesan cheese, browned under the grill
stuffed olives

Tie a band of greaseproof paper firmly round 6 individual soufflé dishes. Mix the cheeses with the mustard and seasonings. Add the aspic jelly and vinegar and leave to get cold. Whip with an electric mixer until frothy but not set. Add the cream cheese to the whipped cream and fold into the mixture, followed by the egg whites. Spoon into the prepared dishes and level the tops. Chill in the refrigerator for several hours.

To serve: remove the papers carefully and press the browned Parmesan cheese round the sides. Garnish with slices of olive.

Serves 6

Iced wine Camembert

METRIC/IMPERIAL/AMERICAN

1 medium ripe Camembert
100–250 ml/4–8 fl oz/½–1 cup white wine
100 g/4 oz/½ cup soft butter
1 tablespoon fine fresh white breadcrumbs
salt and cayenne pepper
50 g/2 oz/½ cup Parmesan cheese, grated
paprika
white grapes, cut into small bunches, to garnish

Scrape most of the rind from the cheese. Pour the wine over the cheese, cover and leave overnight. Lift out the cheese and sieve. Beat with the butter until smooth, adding 2 tablespoons/2 tablespoons/3 tablespoons of the marinating wine and the breadcrumbs. Season well. Turn into a lightly oiled mould, smooth the top, cover and leave to chill for about 3 hours or until firm. Turn out and coat all over with the Parmesan cheese mixed with a little paprika. Set on a flat board or dish.

Cut a circle of greaseproof paper the diameter of the cheese and cut out a design. Lay on top of the cheese and sprinkle with paprika. Remove the paper, being careful not to ruin the design. Arrange the grapes with pretzels, water biscuits and cheese biscuits around the dish.

Serves 4–6

Savoury pears

METRIC/IMPERIAL/AMERICAN
2 thick slices bread with crusts removed, cut into 5-
    mm/¼-inch dice
25 g/1 oz/2 tablespoons butter
1 bunch watercress, washed and chopped
2 ripe dessert pears, peeled, cored and sliced
100 g/4 oz/¼ lb Stilton cheese, crumbled
4 tablespoons/4 tablespoons/⅓ cup double cream
freshly ground pepper
chopped parsley

Fry the diced bread in melted butter until crisp and golden
brown. Place the croûtons in 4 buttered ramekin dishes. Cover
with layers of cress, sliced pears and Stilton cheese. Spoon the
cream over, then sprinkle with pepper and parsley. Cover with
foil and bake in a moderate oven (180°C, 350°F, Gas Mark 4)
for 10–12 minutes. Remove the foil and brown for a few
minutes more. Serve at once, garnished with chopped parsley.

Serves 4

Cheese straw bundles

METRIC/IMPERIAL/AMERICAN
175 g/6 oz/1½ cups plain flour
salt and cayenne pepper
100 g/4 oz/½ cup butter
100 g/4 oz/1 cup dry Cheddar cheese, finely grated

Sift the flour with the seasonings into a bowl and rub in the
butter until the texture of breadcrumbs. Add the cheese, work
the mixture together and knead until smooth. Wrap and chill
for 30 minutes.

Roll out on a floured surface into an oblong 5 mm/¼ inch
thick. Cut out a few circles 4 cm/1½ inches in diameter with a
plain cutter, then using a cutter two sizes smaller, cut out the
centres to form rings. Lift carefully on to a baking sheet. Cut the
remaining pastry into 13–15-cm/5–6-inch long narrow strips.
Lift carefully on to the baking sheet. Cook in a moderately hot
oven (190°C, 375°F, Gas Mark 5) for 10–15 minutes until just
lightly golden brown. Lift carefully on to a wire cooling rack.
When cold, gather the sticks into small bundles and place in
each ring. Arrange on a serving dish and serve with peanuts,
olives, etc., as cocktail savouries.

Serves 4–6

Fork supper dishes

The busy hostess is always on the look-out for new ideas, and there are plenty to choose from in this section. It is important to incorporate dishes which not only look attractive but also ones that offer a choice of flavours and are easy to eat with a fork.

Fork suppers tend to be for larger gatherings of people, so a good selection of food is important. Offer a couple of cold starters and a choice of hot and cold main dishes. Salads are always popular so serve a variety, making full use of colour and texture.

Salade niçoise

METRIC/IMPERIAL/AMERICAN

1 large cucumber
4 tomatoes, skinned, deseeded and diced
350 g/12 oz/$\frac{3}{4}$ lb French beans, cooked and cut into
    2.5-cm/1-inch/1-inch pieces
225 g/8 oz/$\frac{1}{2}$ lb onions, quartered, sliced and blanched
225 g/8 oz/$\frac{1}{2}$ lb green or red peppers, diced
2 (198-g/7-oz/7-oz) cans tuna, drained
French dressing
1 tablespoon chopped fresh herbs – parsley, fennel, basil
1 (56-g/2-oz/2-oz) can anchovy fillets, halved lengthwise
100 g/4 oz/$\frac{2}{3}$ cup black olives, halved and stoned
oil to glaze

Cut a small piece off the cucumber. Peel the remaining cucumber and keep half of this for garnish. Dice the cucumber and mix with the tomatoes, beans, onions, peppers and tuna. Moisten with French dressing and add the herbs. Leave to marinate for 1 hour.

Drain off any excess liquid then spoon on to a flat serving dish and mould to the shape of a fish. Slice the reserved peeled cucumber thinly and surround the salad with slices. Arrange anchovy halves in a lattice pattern as scales. Peel the reserved end piece of cucumber, slice in half and arrange as a tail. Place an olive in the centre of each lattice. Place a halved stuffed olive for an eye, if liked. Brush with a little oil. Serve chilled with hot garlic bread.

Serves 4–6

Festival chicken

METRIC/IMPERIAL/AMERICAN
1 lemon
50 g/2 oz/¼ cup butter
1 (1.75-kg/4-lb/4-lb) roasting chicken, prepared
100 ml/4 fl oz/½ cup white wine
1 small onion, chopped
1 tablespoon oil
1 tablespoon curry powder
150 ml/¼ pint/⅔ cup chicken stock
1–2 tablespoons mango chutney
2 tablespoons/2 tablespoons/3 tablespoons apricot jam
300 ml/½ pint/1¼ cups double cream
150 ml/¼ pint/⅔ cup thick mayonnaise
150 ml/¼ pint/⅔ cup soured cream
chopped red pepper, grapes and cress to garnish

Squeeze the lemon and place the shells with a knob of butter inside the chicken. Place in a roasting tin, spread the remaining butter over the bird and pour some juice and the wine over. Roast in a moderately hot oven (200°C, 400°F, Gas Mark 6) for 25 minutes per 0.5 kg/1 lb. Baste well. Cool, strain off juices.

Soften the onion in the oil. Add the curry powder and cook for 3–4 minutes. Stir in the chicken juices, stock, chutney and jam. Bring to the boil, simmer for 10 minutes, then liquidise or sieve and cool. Whip the cream, add the mayonnaise, soured cream and curry sauce. Season. Add chopped chicken flesh to the sauce. Pile into a dish lined with lettuce and chill. Garnish.

Serves 6

Vitello tonnato

METRIC/IMPERIAL/AMERICAN
1 (56-g/2-oz/2-oz) can anchovy fillets
2 cloves garlic, crushed
1.25 kg/2½ lb/2½ lb boned breast of veal, rolled
100 ml/4 fl oz/½ cup vermouth
freshly ground pepper
1 (198-g/7-oz/7-oz) can tuna, drained
1 large egg yolk
150 ml/¼ pint/⅔ cup oil
300 ml/½ pint/1¼ cups double cream, whipped
lemon juice
1 tablespoon drained capers
stoned black olives and capers to garnish

Mash 6 anchovy fillets and garlic, spread over the veal. Place on foil in a tin, add vermouth and pepper, and package in the foil. Roast in a moderately hot oven (200°C, 400°F, Gas Mark 6) for 1½ hours. Cool.

Mash the tuna with the remaining anchovy fillets to a smooth paste. Add the egg yolk and beat in the oil, a few drops at a time, with an electric mixer. Add cream and enough strained veal liquid to give a coating consistency. Add lemon juice to taste.

Slice the meat and cut into cubes. Mix with the sauce and place in a dish. Sprinkle with capers. Cover and chill in the refrigerator at least overnight. Garnish before serving.

Serves 6

Spinach and herb terrine

METRIC/IMPERIAL/AMERICAN

2 bay leaves
10 rashers lean bacon, thinly sliced
350 g/10 oz/1½ cups frozen chopped spinach, cooked
450 g/12 oz/¾ lb lean belly pork, minced
225 g/8 oz/½ lb sausagemeat
1 onion, finely chopped
2 cloves garlic, crushed
2 teaspoons chopped fresh mixed herbs
2 teaspoons chopped parsley
grated nutmeg
2 eggs, well beaten
175 g/6 oz/¾ cup cooked ham in 5-mm/¼-inch/¼-inch dice
bay leaves to garnish

Grease a 1-kg/2-lb loaf tin. Arrange the bay leaves in the bottom. Flatten the rashers and line the tin.

Mix the spinach, pork, sausagemeat, onion, garlic and herbs well together. Season with salt, freshly ground pepper and nutmeg. Bind with the eggs and turn half the mixture into the prepared tin. Cover with chopped ham and finish with the remaining pork mixture. Press down well. Cover with foil. Place in a roasting tin with water halfway up the sides. Cook in a moderately hot oven (190°C, 375°F, Gas Mark 5) for 2 hours. Lift out of the roasting tin and weight the terrine. Cover and chill in the refrigerator for 24 hours. Turn out of the loaf tin and garnish with bay leaves.

Serves 6–8

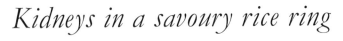

Kidneys in a savoury rice ring

METRIC/IMPERIAL/AMERICAN

50 g/2 oz/¼ cup butter
8 lambs' kidneys, skinned, halved and cored
1 onion, finely chopped
25 g/1 oz/¼ cup flour
300 ml/½ pint/1¼ cups stock
1 teaspoon tomato purée
2 teaspoons Dijon mustard
1 tablespoon Worcestershire sauce
1 tablespoon mushroom ketchup
150 ml/¼ pint/⅔ cup soured cream
chopped parsley to garnish

Melt the butter and sauté the kidneys to brown, remove. Add the onion and cook until soft. Sprinkle in the flour and cook for 1 minute. Add the stock, tomato purée, mustard, Worcestershire sauce and ketchup. Bring to the boil, season to taste and cook for 10 minutes. Add the kidneys and simmer for 20 minutes until the kidneys are tender. Stir in cream. Spoon into the centre of the hot rice ring.

For the rice ring, melt 50 g/2 oz/¼ cup butter in a pan and fry 1 chopped onion until soft. Add 225 g/8 oz/1 cup rice, cooked, and fry for 5 minutes, stirring. Add 225 g/8 oz/8 oz canned sweetcorn, juice of 1 lemon and 1 tablespoon chopped parsley. Season, stir in 1 beaten egg and pack into a buttered ring mould. Press firmly, cover with foil and leave in a cool oven (110°C, 225°F, Gas Mark ¼) for 10–12 minutes. Turn out and garnish.

Serves 4–6

Cannelloni

1 kg/2 lb/2 lb fresh spinach leaves, stalks removed
225 g/8 oz/2 cups button mushrooms, sliced
50 g/2 oz/$\frac{1}{4}$ cup butter
50 g/2 oz/$\frac{1}{4}$ cup cream cheese
salt and freshly ground pepper
grated nutmeg
12 cannelloni
50 g/2 oz/$\frac{1}{2}$ cup finely grated Cheddar and Parmesan
  mixed
parsley sprigs to garnish
BÉCHAMEL SAUCE:
20 g/$\frac{3}{4}$ oz/1$\frac{1}{2}$ tablespoons butter
15 g/$\frac{1}{2}$ oz/2 tablespoons flour
300 ml/$\frac{1}{2}$ pint/1$\frac{1}{4}$ cups flavoured milk
150 ml/$\frac{1}{4}$ pint/$\frac{2}{3}$ cup single cream

Wash the spinach and blanch in boiling salted water for 5 minutes. Drain, press out moisture and chop. Fry the mushrooms in the butter until soft. Add the spinach and cream cheese, season to taste with salt, pepper and nutmeg. Fill the cannelloni, using a piping bag, and lay in a well buttered ovenproof dish. Make up the béchamel sauce (see page 12), then add the cream, season to taste and pour over the cannelloni. Sprinkle with the cheese and bake in a moderate oven (180°C, 350°F, Gas Mark 4) for about 35 minutes until the cannelloni is tender and the cheese browned. Serve garnished with parsley.

Serves 6

Salmon tourtière

200 g/7 oz/$\frac{3}{4}$ cup plus 2 tablespoons butter
2 egg yolks
2–3 tablespoons/2–3 tablespoons/3–4 tablespoons water
275 g/10 oz/2$\frac{1}{2}$ cups plain flour, with a pinch salt
450 g/1 lb/1 lb salmon tail piece, skinned and boned
175 g/6 oz/1$\frac{1}{2}$ cups mushrooms
175 g/6 oz/$\frac{3}{4}$ cup butter, softened
150 ml/$\frac{1}{4}$ pint/$\frac{2}{3}$ cup each single cream and white wine
grated rind of $\frac{1}{2}$ lemon
pinch cayenne pepper and grated nutmeg
2 egg whites, whisked

Work the butter and egg yolks together for pastry, add water, then flour and knead to a smooth paste. Chill for 1 hour.
    Thinly slice one-third of the salmon. Finely mince the remainder with the mushrooms and butter. Add the cream, wine and lemon rind. Add seasonings and fold in egg whites. Line a deep 20-cm/8-inch flan ring with two-thirds of the pastry. Spread half the salmon mixture over and cover with the sliced salmon. Cover with the remaining mixture. Make a lid with the remaining pastry, dampen the edges, position and press firmly together. Decorate with pastry leaves and make a hole in the centre. Brush with egg. Bake in a moderately hot oven (190°C, 375°F, Gas Mark 5) for 35–40 minutes. If liked, add 1 teaspoon mixed herbs to 50 g/2 oz/4 tablespoons melted butter and pour through the centre hole. Garnish and serve.

Serves 6

Seafood pancakes

METRIC/IMPERIAL/AMERICAN
300 ml/½ pint/1¼ cups pancake batter mixture
4 scallops
150 ml/¼ pint/⅔ cup each water and white wine
juice of 1 lemon
225 g/8 oz/1⅓ cups peeled prawns
3 hard-boiled eggs, coarsely chopped
75 g/3 oz/6 tablespoons butter
1 large onion, chopped
175 g/6 oz/1½ cups button mushrooms, quartered
40 g/1½ oz/6 tablespoons plain flour
150 ml/¼ pint/⅔ cup each single and double cream
chopped parsley
25 g/1 oz/¼ cup Parmesan cheese, grated

Make 8–10 thin pancakes and leave to cool; prepare filling.
 Poach the scallops in the water, wine and lemon juice for 5 minutes. Strain and reserve the liquid. Quarter the scallops and mix with the prawns and eggs. Melt the butter and fry the onion and mushrooms until soft. Add the flour and cook for 1 minute then stir in the reserved fish stock and bring to the boil, stirring. Add the single cream, cook gently for 5 minutes then stir in 1 tablespoon parsley and season. Place a spoonful of the mixture on each pancake, roll up and arrange in a greased ovenproof dish. Heat the double cream and spoon over. Sprinkle with the cheese and place in the top of a moderately hot oven (200°C, 400°F, Gas Mark 6) for 10 minutes. Garnish with parsley.

Serves 4

Chicken mille feuille

METRIC/IMPERIAL/AMERICAN
350 g/12 oz/¾ lb puff pastry
BÉCHAMEL SAUCE:
50 g/2 oz/¼ cup butter
50 g/2 oz/½ cup plain flour
450 ml/¾ pint/2 cups flavoured milk
150 ml/¼ pint/⅔ cup single cream
225 g/8 oz/2 cups button mushrooms, sliced
juice of 1 lemon
1 teaspoon dried tarragon
350 g/12 oz/1½ cups cooked chicken, diced
25 g/1 oz/¼ cup Cheddar cheese, grated
tomato slices and cress to garnish

Roll out the pastry thinly and cut into three strips 10 x 30 cm/4 x 12 inches. Lift on to wetted baking sheets, prick and bake in a hot oven (220°C, 425°F, Gas Mark 7) for 15 minutes. Cool.
 Make up the béchamel sauce (see page 12) and keep 150 ml/¼ pint/⅔ cup aside. Sauté the mushrooms quickly in the lemon juice with the tarragon. Mix with the chicken and the remaining sauce. Season.
 Place one pastry sheet on an ovenproof dish and spread with half the chicken mixture. Cover with another layer of pastry and chicken mixture and lay the remaining pastry on top. Press down level with a baking sheet. Spoon over the reserved sauce. Sprinkle with the cheese and place in the top of a moderately hot oven (200°C, 400°F, Gas Mark 6) for 10–15 minutes.

Serves 4–6